D0508137

Coming Off Drugs

James Ditzler is a psychologist who trained in chemical dependence at the internationally renowned Hazelden Foundation in Minnesota and later worked at the Roosevelt Hospital in New York. Since 1975 he has been treating addicts and alcoholics in Britain.

Joyce Ditzler is a state-registered nurse, trained at Guy's Hospital, London. She trained in addiction at the Roosevelt Hospital in New York. She has been treating addicts and alcoholics in Britain since 1975.

Farm Place, which was founded and is run by James and Joyce Ditzler, is a residential treatment centre for addicts and alcoholics, with high success rates.

James Ditzler, MA, Sp.D.Psych.,
and Joyce Ditzler, SRN, RN
with Celia Haddon

COMING OFF DRUGS

MACMILLAN
LONDON

Copyright © James R. Ditzler, Joyce M. Ditzler and Celia Haddon 1986

All rights reserved. No reproduction, copy or transmission of this
publication may be made without written permission. No paragraph
of this publication may be reproduced, copied or transmitted save with
written permission or in accordance with the provisions of the Copyright
Act 1956 (as amended). Any person who does any unauthorised act in
relation to this publication may be liable to criminal prosecution
and civil claims for damages.

First published in Great Britain 1986 by
PAPERMAC
a division of Macmillan Publishers Limited
4 Little Essex Street London WC2R 3LF
and Basingstoke

Associated companies in Auckland, Delhi, Dublin, Gaborone, Hamburg,
Harare, Hong Kong, Johannesburg, Kuala Lumpur, Lagos, Manzini,
Melbourne, Mexico City, Nairobi, New York, Singapore and Tokyo

British Library Cataloguing in Publication Data
Ditzler, James
    Coming off drugs.
    1. Drug abuse — Treatment
    I. Title   II. Ditzler, Joyce   III. Haddon, Celia
    362.2'938   RC564
    ISBN 0-333-41854-9
    ISBN 0-333-41855-7 Pbk

Typeset by Columns of Reading
Printed in Finland by Werner Söderström Oy

Contents

To the six Hs who made our work possible

and also to the thousands of recovering people, their families and friends, who because of the programme must remain anonymous.

Acknowledgements

We would like to thank those people who have helped us during the researching and writing of this book: the Reverend Gordon R. Grimm, Director of Training, and Joan Frederickson, staff librarian, at the Hazeldon Foundation, Minnesota; Mr Michael House, MB, BS, FRCOG, of Charing Cross Hospital, London; Malcolm Lader, DSc, PhD, MD, FRC Psych., DPM, Professor of Clinical Psychopharmacology at the Institute of Psychiatry, London; John Witton, Information Officer at the Institute for the Study of Drug Dependence, London; Mrs Eve Ling and all the staff at Farm Place. In Canada, Australia, New Zealand and South Africa many people helped in the preparation of Appendix 2. Our thanks to them all.

We are particularly grateful to Dr Maurice Lipsedge, M.Phil., FRCP, FRC Psych., Consultant Psychiatrist at the Department of Psychological Medicine, Guy's Hospital, London, who not only gave us invaluable advice but was kind enough to write the introduction to this book.

We are obliged to Alcoholics Anonymous World Services Inc., New York, for permission to reprint the Twelve Steps of AA. We would also like to thank all those recovering addicts and alcoholics, and their families, who shared their experience, strength and hope with us for this book.

Introduction

With drug abuse and alcoholism reaching epidemic proportions, this is a timely book. While the spread of chemical dependence has a variety of causes, the medical and pharmaceutical endorsement of the belief that unhappiness has a pharmacological solution has contributed to the proliferation of tranquilliser and illicit drug abuse over the past twenty-five years. Tranquilliser advertisements have claimed that these chemicals 'have a unique role in helping mankind meet the challenge of a changing world'.

The parents of the young people to whom this book is mainly addressed will recognise that their own reliance on alcohol and pills to suppress unhappiness and conflict has fostered a social climate in which their children have come to expect that chemicals provide an instant panacea. It has been estimated that there are over 100,000 people in Britain who are currently dependent on tranquillisers.

Just as cocaine was promoted by physicians a century ago as a safe cure for morphinism, in recent times a variety of remedies, props, crutches and prescriptions have been offered as solutions to addiction and alcoholism. These 'cures' include aversion therapy, disulfiram implants, opioid antagonists and transcutaneous neural stimulation, in addition to methadone, which was recommended in one psychiatric textbook as a 'proper treatment approach for not only the anxious, irritable and impulsive drug user, but also for young psychopaths of any description' (Thomas P. Detre and Henry G. Jarecki, *Modern Psychiatric Treatment*, J. B. Lippencott Co., Philadelphia and Toronto, 1971).

Each one of these approaches ignores the problem of polyaddiction, which is increasingly the most common pattern of drug abuse, and they all fail to bring about the change in attitude which is fundamental if a return to addiction is to be avoided.

Given the poor success rate of many of the standard approaches, it is perhaps not surprising that a 'legalise heroin' lobby has developed based on the premiss that decriminalisation will eradicate the problem. But this irresponsible pressure group chooses to ignore the damage to the embryo caused by heroin taken during pregnancy. Narcotics cause foetal death and growth impairment. Heroin causes a rate of stillbirth three times the normal. With increasing recognition of the foetal–alcohol syndrome it seems absurd to recommend easy access to another addictive substance that can affect the unborn child.

The treatment programme outlined in this book mobilises the family in a constructive way and teaches alcoholics and addicts to cope with themselves, with other people and with the inevitable stress of daily life without reliance on chemical props. It is to be hoped that this approach will become more widely available throughout the country and within the National Health Service.

Finally, I have had personal knowledge of the Ditzlers' clinical work over the past few years, and their book reflects their own therapeutic style: tough but supportive, confrontative but caring.

Maurice Lipsedge, M.Phil., FRCP, FRC Psych.
London
February 1986

PART ONE

Recovery Is Possible

1

Addicts and Alcoholics: How They Recovered

Drug addicts and alcoholics are not hopeless cases. They can and do get well when they come off and stay off drugs and drink. Thousands of drug addicts and alcoholics have proved this for themselves. No matter what drugs they had been taking, and no matter how severe their addiction was, they have managed to come off drugs and drink and stay off them. They are now leading normal and happy lives.

Since 1969 we have been treating addicts and alcoholics, both as in-patients and out-patients, and we have seen literally thousands of them recover. Our former patients include all kinds of men and women, and by now many of them have been off drugs or drink for up to seventeen years.

We know it can be done. If you are an addict or an alcoholic, you can do it too. If you are the parents or partner of one, take heart – your loved one can do it.

Here are the stories of just some of the addicts and alcoholics we know who are now off drugs and drink, and leading happy and useful lives.

Antony

Antony is a twenty-nine-year-old merchant banker. He went to Eton, then Cambridge University, and then worked in publishing. A *curriculum vitae* shows no signs of his drug-using, yet from university onwards he was injecting heroin and amphetamines.

Antony's mother was a heavy drinker, so from the age of fourteen he was encouraged to drink quite freely at home. In his last two years of school he would wander off to Windsor and drink on his own. Like so many addicts, his first experience of illegal drugs was cannabis, which he smoked at university.

'Several people I knew vaguely from school were using drugs there,' he recalls. 'We all developed a taste for LSD, which livened up a couple of parties. Then came speed.

'My friends at Cambridge were all doing drugs or were the Hooray Henrys who enjoyed seeing others do drugs. But even if I hadn't liked those people, I would have liked the prospect of drugs. The image of rebellion appealed to me. Besides, at the age of fourteen I'd experimented by trying to smoke nutmeg – and that was without any peer pressure at all.'

He found the work at Cambridge difficult because of his heavy drug-using. 'I had a girlfriend whose Daddy was a doctor. He kept large amounts of syringes in the bathroom cupboard, and also ampoules of diamorphine, pethidine, Valium and adrenalin. I tried adrenalin and nearly killed myself. It was in the loo in my parent's house, and I nearly died from it. I only got half of it in.'

Antony managed to leave university with an archaeology and anthropology degree – partly because he stopped drugs in his last term and just drank instead. But he made no preparations for getting a job and finally ended up working as a porter in a department store.

'That first year after leaving Cambridge, my then girlfriend tells me I was doing a *lot* of heroin. Eventually I turned back to speed again.'

Finally, his father used his influence with an old friend to get Antony a job as a sales representative with a publisher, and for the first two years he worked for the firm he was on drugs more or less continuously.

'I stank. I never washed or changed. I don't know what my colleagues thought about me, but the firm didn't seem to notice. Buyers covered up for me because they liked me, and if there was any trouble I could always blame it on the computer, which was always going wrong.

'During those last two years of using drugs I got much nastier withdrawals. Virtually every week I had a serious resolve to stop using drugs. It would last for two or three days and then I'd start again. It wasn't the physical agony which made me start using, but the awful feeling of loneliness. The physical stuff was almost reassuring. It was the mental side of stopping, the despair.'

His family knew something was wrong, but did not think of drugs. When his father discovered some syringes, Antony lied and said that they were there because he was going to draw them! Even when his father sent him to a Harley Street diagnostician, the drugs were not discovered. Antony turned his arms inwards so that the doctor wouldn't see the track marks, and he was never asked about using drugs.

He went back on heroin again. 'Even my dealer told me I stank. There was also the constant fear of the police. I never got registered – it might have interfered with my prospects in life!'

His parents discovered he was on drugs one weekend. He was having a withdrawal fit in his bedroom, and his mother in the room below heard him banging his head on the floor. When she came into his room later and asked if he was OK, Antony said he was. 'But the next morning I chased her round the house crying, "Help me! Help me! Help me! I'm a heroin addict." '

A few days later his father drove him down to a clinic whose treatment philosophy was compatible with the programme of Alcoholics Anonymous and Narcotics Anonymous. 'He spent the whole journey down saying how guilty he was and if only he'd brought me up properly this would never have happened. He was in agonies.'

On arrival, Antony was asked if he had used any mood-altering drugs or if he had been drinking that day. 'I was enraged by this. Of course, we'd stopped off for a couple of pints on the way down! Then Joyce Ditzler came into the room when I was being difficult, refusing to take detox medication from one of the nurses, and said to me: "When are you going to grow up?" '

At first Antony had difficulty in seeing that drink had played a part in his drug-using. 'I hadn't counted drink, you see. I couldn't accept it at first, until somebody made me sit down and tot up how much I drank each day. That was the only way I could see that I was drinking quite a lot, as well as using other drugs.'

The clinic advised his father not to pay off his debts, telling him Antony must do this himself. They told Antony to write to his employers and tell them the truth – that he was having treatment for heroin addiction. The publishers said they would have him back in his job.

'It was a great feeling – not having to con anybody. When all your fears come to light and nothing happens, it makes you feel as if the gates of heaven have opened. When my employers said they'd have me back, I felt extraordinarily good.'

After his stay in the clinic, Antony began going to meetings of Alcoholics Anonymous – every single day at first. 'I could identify with the drinkers because I knew that drink and drugs were basically the same thing. I didn't see any of my old friends – all of them were junkies anyway.

'I spent two more years working for the publishers, going all round the country selling books and going to meetings of AA in faraway places. A process of recovery that I was unaware of was going on. Much of what I got at the clinic and in AA was practical emotional potty-training. If I had a problem we could all laugh about it at meetings, take the piss out of each other and put it back into proper perspective.'

Antony paid off his debts, and when Narcotics Anonymous started up in London he began going to their meetings. He changed from publishing to a job in a merchant bank two years after entering the clinic. Five years later he still goes to NA meetings – in order to make sure he does not go back on drugs or drink.

As a merchant banker he is doing well and has just been sent on a management-development course to further his career. 'We had to take a personality test there. I got ten out of ten for mental health – not bad for a recovering heroin addict!'

Sarah

Married to a top businessman, Paul, Sarah lives in an eighteenth-century rectory in a small village in Hampshire. She is fifty-nine and has two adult children. A mongrel dog, Duke, completes the household.

Her drug-taking, all of it perfectly legal, started when she was twenty-five and working as a physiotherapist in a hospital. The doctor with whom she was working prescribed Sodium Amytal. She took these, or some other barbiturate sleeping pills, continuously for the next twenty-seven years.

'I was totally dependent on them. If I was going on holiday, the sleeping pills would be top of the list of things I had to take with me,' she recalls.

Yet she never abused her pills by taking more than were prescribed – she didn't need to, as doctors were always generous with their prescriptions.

She got married and had two children, both boys. Her marriage was – and still is – a remarkably happy one, except for the years in which drug-using and drink destroyed that happiness.

'I began to use drink to change my feelings around 1968,' recalls Sarah. 'I remember when my older boy was first going to boarding school. He was very homesick, and week after week I'd ring up and be told he was still crying himself to sleep. One night I thought: "I can't bear this, but I've got to phone the school. I know – I'll have a good stiff gin and tonic and then it won't be too bad." '

Over the next two years her drinking became more of a problem. By 1970 her local family doctor confronted her and told her she might be an alcoholic. 'I knew him socially and he saw me about the village. He confronted me on the basis of his observation of me.'

Sarah promptly changed doctors and told all her friends what a lousy GP he had been. Her drinking escalated – a drink at lunchtime, then the odd drink *before* lunchtime, then a drink during the morning to get going. She drank at home secretly and started hiding bottles.

'I didn't have to steal in the ordinary sense, but I stole from my husband. I would go to the local town's department store, buy spirits and then ask them to put it down as other goods on our account. Then I'd tell him I'd been buying presents for people.'

She also started getting medical help – not for her drinking, but for her 'depression'. 'I told my new GP that my problem was depression because my husband was often away on business and my children were away at school.'

Sarah was referred to a psychiatrist who was supposed to know about alcoholism, but she did not tell him about her drinking. He prescribed pills for her depression. 'At various different times I was given barbiturates like Soneryl, Seconal and Tuinal. Then as tranquillisers I had Mogadon and Dalmane, and two kinds of anti-depressants. He just kept trying one thing after another for my depression.'

To check up on her drinking, the psychiatrist had Sarah to stay in his house for a week. She had to arrive at 9 a.m. and stay till 6 p.m. During that week she waited till she got home at night to drink. After seven days of not drinking while she was at his house, the psychiatrist announced: 'Now we've proved you are not an alcoholic!'

Sarah began a round of fee-paying nursing homes. She had electric-shock treatment and hypnotism. The psychiatrist even gave her Duke, the mongrel dog who is now the family pet. 'He said it would help me if I had a dog to love.'

Then her psychiatrist died, and Sarah was transferred to a new one. 'I really conned that man. I used to see him in Harley Street, and I would nip into the ladies loo of a nearby department store with a quarter bottle of vodka before my appointment. Then when he asked about my drinking, I would say it was no problem.' She told him she had lapses of memory and he sent her for a brain scan. She even had an EEG test for epilepsy. 'I didn't know then, but the memory lapses were alcoholic blackouts.'

During this time, the family was beginning to suffer from her drinking. Both boys were at boarding school. 'The older boy began to start not coming home at half-terms and out-weekends. He had excuses like playing in a match, but I knew what it was.' Her husband Paul began to spend more and more time in London, where he had a business flat. 'He felt he couldn't just walk out and leave me.'

Sarah herself felt more and more desperate. Her husband once came home to find her standing on an upstairs window sill threatening to jump. She overdosed twice on pills and booze.

'I felt I couldn't go on,' she says, describing one of her overdoses. 'I could see what I was doing to the family, and I loved them. There was nobody in the house and I didn't think anybody was coming back so I took a handful of barbiturates, and then another and another till I lost consciousness.' Unexpectedly, her husband returned early that day and rushed her to hospital.

By this time Sarah's psychiatrist had realised drink was the problem: a nursing home had discovered a vodka bottle hidden in her handbag. He had tried aversion therapy and Antabuse tablets (which make patients sick when they drink), but both treatments failed. He now recommended Alcoholics Anonymous.

But although Sarah went to AA meetings regularly, she couldn't stop drinking or taking pills. 'The members were always so nice to me, even though I was full of pills or half sloshed at meetings. And it was from them I heard about a clinic whose treatment philosophy was compatible with AA.'

She phoned the clinic herself and booked herself in for the following day. Her psychiatrist warned her that if she stopped taking the pills she was addicted to, she would have problems and might try to commit suicide again.

The clinic gradually took her off alcohol and all her pills, including the barbiturates she had been taking for twenty-seven years. 'I went down there determined to co-operate because I knew it was my last chance. I behaved rather like a schoolgirl at boarding school. I liked the discipline and I felt safe. I told my counsellor everything about myself.'

When she came out of the clinic, Sarah went back to the Alcoholics Anonymous meetings she already knew. She also discovered that her marriage was not lost. 'I didn't know what it would be like. There had been no physical relationship between me and Paul for a couple of years. Maybe Paul would say: "Now you're OK, you get on with it." The first time we made love again, I phoned my counsellor to tell her the good news.'

It took some months for Paul to trust her again, but somehow their marriage survived and now they are happy with each other once more. Sarah still goes to AA meetings to maintain her sobriety and she helps other alcoholics to become sober themselves.

Jane

In only three years of using illegal drugs, Jane, the privileged daughter of a wealthy businessman, was reduced to stealing and living in squats. Today, five years after coming off drugs, she has regained her health and happiness. Aged twenty-six, she is married with a two-year-old daughter, Sophie. She runs her own dress shop.

Jane's use of drink and drugs started at the age of thirteen. She was expelled from boarding school for having a flask of gin under her school uniform, but despite this and a further expulsion from a second school, she managed to complete several O- and A-levels.

'I had feelings of inadequacy from a very young age,' she remembers. 'I appeared full of confidence yet I was always seeking attention. I was always telling fibs, like saying I had two ponies at home when I didn't. I always wanted to be cool and to be in with the right gang.'

Her parents' marriage started slowly to break up when she was fourteen. 'It upset me a lot. If I had talked about it many of the bad feelings would have gone away. But I didn't discuss it with anyone. I was unable to express my feelings.'

Jane's drug-taking started at the age of eighteen when she left school and went to London. 'I was immediately attracted to the druggy set. I thought it was glamorous. It appealed to me because I thought it was terribly romantic. I wasn't friendly with the kind of responsible people who were doing secretarial courses.'

Three months after arriving in London, she had taken almost all the illegal drugs – starting with cannabis, then cocaine and heroin. 'The drugs gave me the ability not to care. I always said I didn't care, but I did. Heroin calmed me down.'

That autumn Jane fell in love with a young man at university and they started taking heroin together. After three months of using, however, her boyfriend decided he had had enough. 'I said I was going to give up too, and I did want to, but I couldn't. You know, I really do believe in the disease concept of addiction, because when I started drugs I plummeted like a stone.'

A few months later Jane began the search for something that would help her stop. She told her parents and they too began a series of rescue attempts. She had the black-box treatment twice – to no avail. She had psychoanalysis to help the underlying problems. She was put in a private psychiatric hospital in France for nine months. 'I picked up all the loony habits quickly. If things were dull, I would start throwing flowerpots and the other patients would imitate me. Then I'd be given a big injection of Largactil into my bottom. It used to make me dribble and make my tongue hang out.'

After that, Jane registered with a London hospital for methadone treatment and at one point her parents hired a series of private nurses to look after her at home. 'My parents paid my debts, bought me new clothes, sent me on holidays, and then sent me to New York. It was meant to be a new life with a new flat.'

In New York she overdosed on PCP and had two cardiac arrests. Her father had to fly out to her, not knowing if she would be alive or dead on his arrival. 'He told me later he was so desperate about me that after yet another terrible phone call about me he knelt down on the office floor and begged God to let me die.'

Then Jane's parents were advised to stop trying to rescue her. While she was living at home and using drugs, her mother called the police. 'They busted me in her house. She had to do it to protect my younger brother, who was also living there.'

Without her parents' care, she got rapidly worse. 'I was dossing anywhere and it didn't matter who with. I had stolen from my parents and I'd done a bit of minor burglary from friends. I was so bad, I would sit in the bath with cold water. I'd have a couple of grams of cocaine and overdose. Then I'd come round and immediately reach for the syringe and start again. *The cold water was to bring me round for another shot.*'

Finally she was put into hospital under the mental-health laws as a 'danger to her own life'. Her parents visited her there with a GP who knew of a clinic whose treatment philosophy was compatible with the programme of Narcotics Anonymous and Alcoholics Anonymous. For a year Jane was treated first in the clinic itself, then in a halfway house nearby. 'I was so crazy and my brain was so fuddled I don't remember much about it at first. I never felt like walking out and I never had severe cravings. I was beyond all that.

'I think I responded to the straight talk I got from my counsellor. I don't take much notice of subtlety. I'm straight up and I like people who are straight up with me. The no-bullshit approach was a good tactic with me.'

When she first moved into the halfway house, Jane started going to Narcotics Anonymous meetings every day. 'I wanted to be in with the right set, but this time it *was* the right set. I had no other friends left.

'At first all I wanted was to be a cook at the clinic, and then get well enough to be a counsellor myself. I gave it my life, my soul, my everything. I loved it there. I also had a lot of fear and terror about going back to London.'

When Jane did move back to London she shared a flat with a non-drug-using girlfriend. She did the secretarial course she had once despised. Then she met Andrew, the young businessman who is now her husband. 'At first he questioned my continued attendance at NA and the fact that I must not drink. But I wouldn't budge. I said: "NA is first. Not you." It was a big challenge for him, and anyway, he likes difficult women!'

A year later, when they married, Andrew had gone to NA meetings with Jane and had come to admire the recovering addicts for the way they helped each other and those still using drugs. He had also gone to Families Anonymous meetings, where the families of addicts support each other.

Nowadays, Jane's life is a full one: she has a child and her own fashion shop. Yet she is still committed to Narcotics Anonymous. 'In the first year of recovery I was obsessive about being a recovering addict, but this programme is a path to normal living and now I lead what I think is a thoroughly normal life.'

Harry

Harry is a forty-six-year-old magazine columnist. He is at the top of his profession, well known not just in this country but in the United States too. He is divorced with two young children whom he sees regularly. A very talented man, he managed to continue his writing throughout his time as an addict. Perhaps the only sign that things weren't quite right was that he would write for money things that he did not believe in. Yet, for all the drugs he was taking, the quality of his work was still competent. He was making a great deal of money and never had any shortage of freelance work from magazines and newspapers both in Britain and in the United States.

For Harry, addiction started with alcohol. He was a heavy drinker from the word go, and as a student occasionally took amphetamines.

'I was introduced to marijuana in New York by a black writer, and I thought it was really heavy. To get it, we had to go down to Greenwich Village and knock three times and ask for Charlie.'

His career began to suffer from his drinking. Harry married another drinker and they would have fierce rows, culminating in his beating her up. Divorce followed. Then, around the late 1960s, he joined Alcoholics Anonymous and gave up alcohol altogether.

But Harry didn't give up marijuana, despite AA's recommendation that members should avoid all mood-altering drugs. 'In my back pocket, so to speak, I had drugs. I had hashish, LSD, Mandrax and Tuinal on which I once OD'd. I thought the AAs were too simple-minded to know about this.'

In the next thirteen years cannabis became more and more important to him. 'I lived virtually constantly on hashish. I'd roll a joint first thing when I woke up in the morning. I'd smoke it all day and all night, and the only anxiety I ever had was when I ran out of it!'

He was still getting good journalistic work, but more and more his life was given over to smoking cannabis. He married again and had two children.

'One of the saddest things about my whole hashish time was the inability to play with my children, because I actually really did love those babies. But I couldn't get out of my head-trip to play with them.

'My life became really inward-looking, self-feeding and feeding an imagination which went round and round in circles. I wanted to write novels, I wanted to write poetry, I wanted to write books. I wanted to express myself like crazy but I couldn't because I was stuck in this hash habit. It had me completely in thrall.'

Harry's last few days on drugs were spent in Miami, where he was researching a series of articles for an American magazine. Ironically, he was still going to Alcoholics Anonymous meetings. 'I arrived in Miami and I called AA, and then I called the guy with the drugs and I scored a lot of drugs. I finished up in a hotel room in Miami with a lot of Columbian flowerheads grass which is very trippy and very strong, and also something masquerading as cocaine, which I suspect was sulphate, and something masquerading as mescaline, which I also suspect was sulphate. I sat in the hotel room fantasising and watching all-night colour TV and getting high and stoned.'

The following day Harry went to an AA meeting and for the first time heard someone claiming to be 'an addict and an alcoholic'. Yet for a couple more days and nights he locked himself in his hotel room, fantasising and taking drugs. 'In the middle of the night I got into awful despair, and I prayed, and I think I meant it.'

A girl he had met through AA rang him the next day, and asked him if he was coming to another AA meeting. 'I can't because I've got a drug problem' was Harry's reply. The words just seemed to pop out of his mouth, despite himself. It was the first time he had admitted it to anybody.

The girl laughed. 'That's fine,' she said. 'Can you get through the lobby?'

Harry burst into tears. 'I don't think anybody but another addict would have asked that question. Because nobody but an addict knows how paranoid you can get in a hotel room. You can be on the street or in the room, but you cannot get through the lobby because the guy on the desk will *know*.'

Harry flushed all his drugs down the toilet. He had a bath. And that night he went to his first meeting of Narcotics Anonymous. When he realised where he was being taken, he objected at first, saying he wasn't into narcotics. The NA members who had come to fetch him asked: 'What have you been using?'

He said: 'Well, only . . .'

And they all chorused: 'Marijuana and cocaine, right?' They asked him how long he had been using them, and for the first time Harry counted up the years. They came to thirteen. 'Thirteen years constitutes a habit, right?' they said to him.

'I think it was the proudest time in my life, because I felt that I really belonged with the kind of heavy dudes I always wanted to belong to. I had been overwhelmed with the feeling that I wasn't a drug addict because I was only a hash addict and not a heroin addict.'

Back in London there were no Narcotics Anonymous meetings like there are now. Harry went back to Alcoholics Anonymous, and every time he spoke he described himself as an 'alcoholic and an addict'. Slowly, other AA members who had had a problem with drugs as well as with drink heard about him and got in touch. A year later, in 1979, they formed the first Narcotics Anonymous meeting in London.

But Harry's first year off drugs was a difficult one. He had returned home to London to find that his second wife had fallen in love with somebody else. He realised, too, that he didn't love her.

'My first major problem was how to relieve myself of my family with the least pain to the children and to their mother. The work I did on that separation was the only work I'd ever put into a relationship in my life, and the day that I sat at Julia's wedding to the man who is now stepfather to my kids was the first time I had ever felt like a man. A grown-up man.'

That was some time ago. Harry has now been off drugs for seven years. Most people never knew he was on them in the first place, but his colleagues notice that his writing is better. He has written and had published the novel he used just to talk about.

Sometimes he hears people talking about cannabis as if it isn't a drug that can make people into addicts. 'If anybody thinks you cannot be addicted to hashish, they've got another think coming,' is all he says.

Ricky

Ricky lives in a small flat in one of London's high-rise blocks. It is decorated with American-Indian objects, patterned rugs and several houseplants. He is thirty-eight years old, born and bred in London, and has never been married. Indeed, his background is one of deprivation and difficulties. He was brought up in a children's home and was in trouble with the law by the time he was eight. At the age of fifteen he was given a suitcase and a bank book containing £10, and thrown out of the children's home.

He doesn't blame his addiction on his background. 'It doesn't make me different. I think in a lot of ways I was better off. I had a lot of brothers and sisters.'

What is remarkable, however, is how Ricky managed to recover without any of the help that money or class connections can give. He beat his drug addiction the hard way – but he succeeded. Today, he has been clean and sober for six years.

He started drinking and taking drugs as a teenager, using amphetamines, 'which I really enjoyed. I used to see heroin addicts, and I used to think "No, I'll never end up like that." '

Then, with a girlfriend, he moved into a house where some heroin addicts lived in the top-floor flat. They were getting heroin from a doctor who freely prescribed what addicts wanted. 'So for a while I was skin-popping heroin. It was just like amphetamines except that you got a bigger effect and it lasted a lot longer and, amazingly enough, you didn't come down.'

Using a needle to mainline the drugs into his veins followed a few months later. 'Within a year I was heavily addicted to heroin and I was mainlining. I started injecting a lot, at least four to six times a day.'

When he was twenty, Ricky had his first treatment in a National Health Service drug-dependence unit. He had a fix before he turned up to see the doctor, who asked him what he was taking. Ricky told him a huge amount of heroin.

At this point Ricky realised he was not going to be admitted to the hospital, but just registered as an addict. The doctor simply wrote out a prescription for heroin with methadone. 'He gave me the amount I said I took. I injected it and I was acting quite normally in front of him so I got a very, very big script. But of course you don't really sort of last long on it. You never go by the book with it, you know.

'On methadone it's like you're walking around in a sleep, in a daze, because you're just existing. You talk to most addicts – all they live for is the chemist in the morning, when they can get their methadone. It never works anyway.'

In theory, the doctor was going to cut down over the weeks the amount of drugs Ricky was taking. But Ricky never kept his appointments, and one Saturday he turned up to find that the doctor had not left a prescription for him. 'So I had a big row with him and that was the end of being with him.'

His life became a series of encounters with the police. 'I did all the usual things, the street things, like robberies and God knows what else for drugs. I was crazy.' Often he had to go through cold-turkey withdrawal in a police cell.

At the age of twenty-one he served his first prison sentence. When he came out he tried to stay off drugs: 'I tried for three weeks. I felt really vulnerable. I didn't know whether I was coming or going. I didn't fit in anywhere. I didn't know what to do.'

The only way he knew how to cope was to use drugs again. In 1972 he got himself re-registered as an addict, while he was on the run from the police. 'I was barred from certain hospitals because I was known as a violent, unpredictable addict. I got put into this hospital because I had an abscess on my arm and it was getting so bad that they were thinking of taking my arm off.' He was given methadone there, then passed on to another hospital which gave him heroin again. 'I thought, "That's crazy. Right now I'm on methadone and now they're going to register me for heroin", which they did. Only this time they had got wiser. They were cutting me down very quickly.'

Like other addicts, Ricky supplemented his prescription with heroin bought on the street. 'They didn't know that, but they know that most addicts do it anyway.'

That year he was arrested for possession of black-market heroin and was given a prison sentence of eighteen months. 'That's when I took a good look at myself. A lot of people were dying and that frightened me. And also, with heroin, like any drug, you get so far with it and you don't get high any more. So I was fed up with that.'

When he came out of prison, Ricky went to a unit for drug addicts. 'It was the kind of place where you scream and shout at each other. I went through all that. But it was a protected environment. As soon as I got out on the streets and started living I felt those old feelings come back and I didn't know what to do. I just followed those feelings.'

The unit had told him it was all right to drink, so he drowned the feelings with alcohol rather than drugs. 'I didn't believe that I would get hung up on alcohol, but I did. I ended up for about five years living on park benches going insaner and insaner and insaner.'

He was in and out of prison on drunk-and-disorderly charges. One of the magistrates he appeared before gave him the number of Alcoholics Anonymous, but Ricky didn't want to know.

It was his mother, whom he hadn't known as a child, who got through to him. She turned up in his life, together with brothers and sisters, and Ricky spent several weekends with her. 'I was leading a double life. They didn't know I was sleeping rough in parks.'

One weekend his mother told him, 'If you come back any drunker we won't let you in.' Nothing that Ricky had gone through – the beatings, police cells, prisons or hospitals – had got through to him. But that weekend his mother did. He went to a pub, cried for hours, then rang up the Samaritans. They suggested Alcoholics Anonymous. Ricky rang AA and a man came out to visit him. 'He travelled several miles to see me. I respected that.'

Ricky stopped drinking. He walked five miles to his nearest Alcoholics Anonymous meeting, picking up cigarette ends on the way. 'I was beaten, in the face, in the arm, through fighting. I said to them, "Well, I'm here. I'm not drinking. But I used to be a heroin addict." '

For the next three months he went to an AA meeting every day. The only thing that distressed him was that there was no chance to talk about his drug addiction. Then he went to an AA meeting and heard people talk about being glad to be sober, and he thought: 'Do I have to take all this?' He told them how he felt and went straight round to the pub and got drunk.

That was his last drink. Since then he has never taken any drug – neither illegal drugs nor prescribed drugs like tranquillisers. A few months later, he heard Harry talking at an AA meeting about being both an alcoholic and an addict, and when Narcotics Anonymous started up in London he went to their meetings.

Ricky started getting involved in NA and in helping addicts get off drugs. He went back to the magistrate who had told him about Alcoholics Anonymous and told him about the existence of Narcotics Anonymous. They had dinner together. He went back to the clinic where he had been treated, and told the doctor there how he was staying off drugs with the help of NA. He even went as an NA delegate to the United States NA Conference – getting a US visa with difficulty, because of his criminal record.

'I learned a lot in NA. I learned to grow up. I didn't know before, but I was pretty immature. I had a chip on my shoulder. Today I haven't got that, or I hope I haven't. I try and be gentle. I try and be loving.

'For me, going to that conference was the impossible dream. It proved that NA works. I was written down as a hopeless case,' says Ricky. 'I came from the gutter. By the end there wasn't a treatment centre that would have me – but Narcotics Anonymous did.'

If you are a drug user reading this book, you may say to yourself 'I'm not that bad, because I never went to prison.' Or you may feel you are different because you do not use drugs in exactly the same way, or you do not use exactly the same combination of drugs. Or perhaps you are an alcoholic who has never used illegal drugs at all.

All drug addicts and alcoholics are slightly different, just as all individuals are. But what they have in common are the feelings they experience as drug and alcohol dependence tightens its grip on them. If you cannot decide whether you are an addict or an alcoholic, you will find it helpful to turn straight to Chapter 4.

Others who read the stories above may be surprised to discover how the addicts were usually taking not just one but several drugs. They may also be surprised to discover that alcohol played a part in their addiction.

But these stories reflect a basic truth – drug dependence is not a tidy illness. Most addicts will use whatever drug is available, falling back on alcohol or prescribed drugs if they cannot get the drug they like best. We believe that drug dependence and alcoholism are all part of the same illness, which we call chemical dependence. Chapter 4 explains this more clearly. Chapter 11 gives some help to those whose work brings them into contact with addicts and outlines the effectiveness of our treatment.

Friends and families who worry in case someone they love may have a drug or drink problem will find Chapters 2 and 3 helpful – to find out more about the illness of drug dependence and what they can do about it.

PART TWO

For Family and Friends

2

What Drugs Do

The good news is that drug addicts can recover from their illness of drug dependence – if they choose. The bad news is that staying on drugs will make them even more ill than they are already.

The drugs that addicts take are ones which alter the mood. They artificially change the feelings of those who take them – either elevating the emotions, tranquillising them, sedating them or producing varying states like euphoria and hallucinations. But these mood-altering drugs taken by addicts cost the users more than money. There is a price to pay in return for the pleasure they initially give. And that price can be very high indeed.

Drug users often do not know what the drugs are doing to them, or the price they are paying. There is often a kind of snobbery in the drug world, which makes addicts look down on those who do not use what they consider the truly 'in' drugs.

Asking addicts about drugs is as sensible as asking five-year-olds about sweets. They can tell you what they like and they can also tell you what it does for them. But they may have little idea about how drugs damage the human body and mind – before it's too late.

Besides, addicts – and sometimes even those who treat them – fall for myths about drugs. All the stories about 'soft' drugs being safe, or how 'hard' drugs don't matter if they are not injected, probably started life as drug dealers' propaganda and are continued by addicts who do not want to face reality.

There is only one truth. *There is no such thing as a completely safe mood-altering drug.*

The first stage in doing something about drug dependence is to learn a little bit more about the drugs themselves.

Drugs that cause dependence

The drugs that make people into addicts have one thing in common: all of them affect the mood. Most of them – drugs like heroin, cocaine or cannabis – begin by creating a feeling of pleasure in the mind. That is why people take them.

Sometimes this pleasure-feeling isn't very strong. Drugs like tranquillisers, for instance, don't so much give pleasure as take away pain. These pills help ward off unpleasant feelings, such as anxiety and fear.

But the mood-altering drugs do more than just give pleasure or take away pain. They have their own dangers. There may be side-effects which damage body and mind. There is also the very real danger of creating dependence. We shall look at this in more detail in Chapter 4.

You will notice that this book is not just about heroin and other illegal drugs. It also deals with drugs like tranquillisers, which are legally prescribed by doctors, and about that other mood-altering drug, alcohol, which is legally available. Addiction, which we usually call chemical dependence, can involve these drugs as well as the illegal drugs.

Some dangers of drug-taking

All mood-altering drugs in some way distract the user from reality. Taken excessively, as addicts use them, there are obvious dangers. When people are drunk on alcohol, stoned on cannabis or out of their mind on cocaine or heroin, they are, for instance, vulnerable to road accidents, falls and other accidental injuries. Even small amounts of drugs like tranquillisers or alcohol can affect their ability to drive or operate machinery.

All drugs become more dangerous when they are mixed. Adding one drug on top of another increases the chances of overdose. Mixed together, lower doses of either drug are more powerful and will prove fatal earlier.

Finally, all drugs bought on the street are a potential danger because they may not be what they claim to be. Many are mixed with other substances to give them more bulk. Sometimes these substances are harmful in themselves. They may be stronger than claimed, making accidental overdose a possibility.

The following are the most common mood-altering drugs that cause dependence. Each has slightly different risks.

Heroin

Street names: Chinese, Dragon, H, Henry, Horse, Junk, Skag, Smack.

Heroin is an opiate, the name given to drugs derived from the opium poppy. In legitimate medicine it acts as a strong painkiller, but almost all the heroin that finds its way on to the streets is illegally imported.

At first heroin may make the user feel sick or vomit, but these side-effects soon pass. Euphoria and a relaxed detachment are the pleasurable feelings the drug produces.

It is highly addictive, whether it is sniffed, smoked or injected. The idea that smoking or sniffing heroin is less likely to cause addiction than injecting is drug dealers' propaganda.

How it is used

1. *Snorted*. It is sniffed up the nose.

2. *Inhaled*. This is called 'chasing the dragon'.

3. *Injected*. This is not always easy, as veins collapse under such treatment.

How often

A heroin addict needs a dose every two to four hours, depending upon the amount and purity of the drug and the personal tolerance of the addict. Some addicts may need to take the drug even more often. If the addict is using a combination of cocaine and heroin – 'a snowball' – injections will need to be more frequent.

In the early stages of the illness, addicts can stop quite easily for a few days or even a few weeks. But without proper help they will always start again.

Health risks

In itself, heroin is not as damaging to the body or brain as some other drugs. These are the risks.

1. *Lifestyle*. Addicts stop looking after themselves. Poor food and bad hygiene make them vulnerable to disease. Crime and prostitution to pay for drugs have obvious risks.

2. *Injecting*. Shared needles carry the risks of hepatitis and AIDS. Dirty needles or adulterated heroin damages veins and arteries and can produce blood clots, abscesses, massive infections of the limbs and damage to the valves of the heart.

3. *Overdose*. This is likely to occur when the addict is injecting. The heroin may be stronger than expected. Or, after a gap in using, tolerance has changed. Many addicts claim they will never inject. Most, but not all, eventually do, if they carry on using heroin long enough.

4. *Emotional damage*. Addicts suffer from self-pity, despair, hopelessness and irrational resentments.

Other opiates and narcotic analgesics

As well as heroin, there are other opiates, such as morphine, Diconal (dipipanone), Temgesic (buprenorphine) and methadone (of which more later). There are also narcotic analgesics, such as codeine and DF 118 (dihydrocodeine tartrate). These all have legitimate medical uses, but are also used by addicts if they cannot get more favoured drugs.

They may be swallowed, or crushed and injected. The dangers are similar to those of heroin. Diconal, when it is injected, is particularly dangerous.

Methadone

Methadone (brand name Physeptone) is a drug which is often used to treat heroin addicts. It is a synthetic drug similar to opiate drugs, which was originally developed, and is still used, as a painkiller in legitimate medicine.

Methadone has less of a euphoric effect and gives more of a zombie-like feeling than heroin. It is also longer lasting – from twelve to twenty-four hours. It is highly addictive. Many heroin addicts 'treated' with methadone become methadone addicts.

As methadone is legally prescribed, addicts could until recently get it relatively easily from some drug-dependence clinics. Unfortunately, it is much more difficult to withdraw people from methadone than from heroin.

Methadone is also frequently sold on the streets by addicts who then use the money to buy heroin or their favourite drug.

How it is used

Methadone is now usually prescribed in a syrup to swallow and less frequently in ampoules to inject.

How often

Most addicts on methadone are prescribed a dose which they collect at intervals and then use when they need it.

Health risks

1. *Overdose.* If used in the prescribed quantities, methadone is not likely to produce an overdose. Even so, with addicts this is unpredictable. Mixed with illegal drugs (a common practice among addicts), it can prove fatal.

2. *Abnormal functioning.* Addicts assume they are doing better on methadone, yet they are not really functioning normally. In that sense, methadone may delay their recovery.

Cocaine

Street names: Coke, Snow.

Derived from the leaves of the coca plant, cocaine reaches the streets as a white powder. It is often diluted with talcum powder or dried milk, sometimes with more dangerous additives.

It acts as a stimulant on the brain, producing euphoria and excitement. Blood pressure rises, breathing becomes rapid and shallow. This is shortly followed by a down period of depression. Addicts often crave repeated doses to stave off the down feelings.

Cocaine is highly addictive, despite claims to the contrary. Because of its undeserved reputation as a harmless drug, and its jet-set image, cocaine can wreak more damage than heroin.

How it is used

1. *Snorted*.

2. *Inhaled*. It is sometimes smoked in cigarettes.

3. *'Freebasing'*. The powder is prepared, then smoked or inhaled. This is a particularly dangerous way of taking cocaine.

4. *Injected*. This maximises the effect of the drug.

5. *Swallowed*. This is the least popular method.

How often

Cocaine leaves the body rapidly, therefore addicts need to top up frequently if they are to avoid the down feeling that will follow.

In the early stages of their illness, cocaine addicts may be weekend users, or may have relatively long periods off the drug. This discontinuous pattern of using cocaine does not necessarily mean they are in control of their habit, since episodes get closer together.

Health risks

1. *Lifestyle*. Like the heroin addict, the cocaine addict stops looking after himself or herself. This effect of the drug might be slower with cocaine than with heroin.

2. *Paranoia* is common among regular users. Hallucinations can also follow. Fits can occur when cocaine is freebased. Psychotic behaviour can result from relatively small doses. These are symptoms of the mental illness this drug can produce relatively early in the user.

3. *Snorting* the drug can destroy the septum (the wall dividing the two halves of the nose) and long-term freebasing can cause deterioration of the lung tissue.

4. *Injecting* carries different risks from injecting heroin. A sudden rise in blood pressure can cause bleeding in the brain and heart attacks.

5. *Overdose*. There is only a thin line between the amount of cocaine used for euphoria and the amount that will cause acute cocaine poisoning. If the dose is high enough, the drop in blood pressure as the cocaine wears off can kill.

Amphetamines and other stimulants

Street names: Speed, Billy (short for Billy Whizz), French Blues, Uppers, Dexies, Black Bombers, Black and Whites, Green and Browns.

Amphetamine sulphate comes both in powder and pill form, thus many of the street names refer to the colours of the tablets. Apisate or Tenuate Dospan (diethylpropion) and Ritalin (methylphenidate) are drugs with a similar effect.

Amphetamine, like cocaine, has a stimulant effect, producing a feeling of euphoria and excitement. Breathing and heartrate speed up.

How it is used

1. *Snorted.*

2. *Swallowed.*

3. *Injected.*

4. *Drunk.* The powder is dissolved in water and drunk. This is not a common method.

How often

Like cocaine, the euphoria and excitement produced by the drug are followed by a down period. Regular users may have to take increasing doses to attain the same feeling.

In the early stages of the illness, amphetamine addicts alternate periods of using the drug with periods off it. As their dependence progresses, they sometimes use tranquillisers or alcohol to bring themselves down.

Health risks

1. *Lifestyle.* Amphetamines literally use up those who use them. Both hunger and fatigue vanish when the drug is used, so lack of sleep and food lowers resistance to disease.

2. *Hallucinations, delusion and paranoia* develop among regular users. 'Amphetamine psychosis' can develop.

3. *Heart attacks and damaged blood vessels* can result in those who use the drug and take strenuous exercise.

4. *Injecting* has the same risks as injecting heroin.

Glue sniffing, solvents, etc.

All kinds of household substances (for obvious reasons we shall not be explicit) are sniffed. They give the user a feeling rather like drunkenness. They can be sedating or disinhibiting, or can produce distortions of reality.

Sniffing is not highly addictive, but some kids nevertheless become dependent on it. Others experiment for only a short time. Glue sniffing may be the prelude to trying other drugs.

Health risks

1. *Suffocation*. Using large plastic bags or sniffing in confined spaces can mean breathing is obstructed. Users can also choke on their own vomit. Some gases squirted directly into the mouth produce suffocation.

2. *Heart attacks* can be caused by inhaling some solvents.

3. *Brain damage, fits, liver and kidney damage* – these can all result from prolonged or intense sniffing.

Cannabis

Street names: Pot, Grass, Hash, Weed, Dope, Ganja, Blow, Bush, Splif (a cannabis cigarette), Tea.

Cannabis comes from a bushy plant, which can be grown in Britain. Herbal cannabis, known as marijuana, is the dried leaves of the plant. 'Hash' is a resin from the plant pressed into blocks. Cannabis occasionally comes in the form of cannabis oil, a liquid produced from the resin. This is rare in Britain.

The hippies of the Sixties, now middle-aged, claimed cannabis was not addictive. They were wrong. Though it is not as addictive as heroin, cannabis certainly has its addicts.

It also acts as the gateway to other drugs. Not everybody who smokes cannabis goes on to try heroin. But almost all heroin addicts started on pot.

How it is used

1. *Smoked*. Using cigarette papers, cannabis is mixed with tobacco and smoked like a cigarette. Or it can be smoked in a pipe known as a 'chillum'.

2. *Eaten or drunk*. Occasionally cannabis is baked in a cake or mixed with liquid and drunk.

Health risks

1. *Bronchitis and lung disease* result from smoking cannabis faster than from smoking tobacco. Not enough research has been done for definite conclusions to be reached, but some research already suggests that cannabis may produce lung cancer.

2. *The reproductive system* in both men and women is badly affected by cannabis, producing a low sperm count, low levels of the male hormone in men, and sometimes early menopause in women.

3. *Resistance to disease* may be lowered by cannabis, and the body's immune response system may be disrupted.

4. *Mental disturbances* may be produced in long-term users. Despite the Sixties' propaganda, this is not a safe drug.

LSD and hallucinogenic mushrooms

Street names: Acid, magic mushrooms.

LSD, or lysergic acid diethylamide, is a white powder that may be sold in pill form or as a small square of blotting paper impregnated with the drug. Its effects will depend on the user's mood. Bad trips are a possibility.

How they are used

1. *Swallowed* as tablets or blotting paper squares.

2. *Eaten and drunk*. Mushrooms are cooked and eaten, or made into a kind of mushroom tea.

How often

LSD is not normally used daily, but in occasional doses. It is often part of a pattern of general drug experimentation and use.

Health risks

1. A bad 'trip' can result in intense anxiety and panic. This is particularly likely to happen to young and immature users.

'Flashbacks' can also occur. This is a sudden return to the hallucinatory experience days or even months later.

2. *Psychotic reactions* are a serious risk.

3. *Poisoning.* If the wrong kind of mushroom is picked, severe poisoning can result. Some of the British fungi can kill even if only a little is eaten.

PCP or phencyclidine

Street names: Angel Dust, Monkey Dust, Rocket Fuel, Crystal Cyclone, Peace Pill, Supergrass.

This is an appalling drug, which is often mistaken for LSD or sold as cannabis. It comes either as a white powder, or as tablets or capsules, or with leafy substances designed to be smoked in cigarettes. It may also be sold as a mixture with other drugs.
   Its legitimate use is in veterinary medicine, not for humans. In low doses it gives a drunken feeling with numbed extremities and general incoordination, and in higher doses it leads to unconsciousness.

How it is used

It can be injected, smoked or snorted.

How often

It is not commonly used continuously because of its unpredictable and unpleasant side-effects, but very occasionally an individual starts using it on a daily basis.

Health risks

1. *Numbing.* Even in small doses this drug causes the body to feel numb. Users may therefore burn or maim themselves while under its influence. They may also hurt others while under its influence, because it can make users extraordinarily strong and violent.

2. *Coma and unconsciousness* can be caused by even moderate doses. There is also a halfway stage where the user is experiencing acute emotional turmoil but *cannot speak*.

3. *Schizophrenia-like reactions, paranoia and permanent memory loss* and other severe consequences can result from high doses. A user

can flicker in and out of coma for months at a time after a high dose.

4. *Acute psychological disorders* lasting for years are among the side-effects of heavy use. Chronic users may lose the ability to tell direction – thus they may drown in a few inches of water because they do not know they are lying face down in it. People using PCP sometimes jump off buildings or stand in front of traffic because they think they have superhuman powers. Horror stories really do apply to this drug.

5. *Overdosing* is common, because this drug is taken in the mistaken belief that it is LSD or some other drug.

Tranquillisers and sleeping pills

Daytime minor tranquillisers and night-time sleeping pills are interchangeable, all members of the benzodiazepine family of drugs. (For the many brand names involved see Appendix 1.) In the past these were prescribed in large quantities for months at a time, which sometimes stretched into years.

These drugs do not give much pleasure, but they do diminish pain. Feelings of anxiety, and indeed feelings in general, are damped down by them. Most of the sleeping pills exert a tranquillising effect through the following day.

Tranquillisers are addictive. These pills are so readily available from doctors that it is barely necessary to buy them on the street. Nor are they very popular among addicts who use illegal drugs – except when no other drugs are available or to mix with other drugs.

However, they are popular with alcoholics, who often become dependent upon a mixture of alcohol and these pills. There are also thousands of tranquilliser addicts who have become dependent on these drugs without an accompanying drink problem thanks to their own ignorance of the dangers and their doctors' generous prescribing. They are as much drug addicts as those who take heroin. The only difference is that the medical profession has been slow to recognise the extent of the problem and its damaging effect on patients, families, work and driving ability.

Health risks

1. *Overdose*. Though they are relatively safe on their own,

tranquillisers can kill when they are mixed with alcohol or other drugs.

2. *Brain damage*. Research is still going on to see if tranquillisers taken over a long period of time can produce brain damage.

3. *Withdrawal problems* produced by these drugs last for many months and can be disabling, mimicking the symptoms for which the drugs were originally prescribed. This increases the fear and anxiety of the patient, who feels that the original problem still exists.

Barbiturates

Street names: Barbs, Dolls.

These were once popular sedatives and sleeping pills, used in the same way as tranquillisers are nowadays. But because they are so dangerous in overdose, they have been largely phased out in legitimate medicine.

Barbiturates are still available on the street. On the whole, they give slightly more of a drunken feeling than tranquillisers, though their effect is more to blot out mental pain than to give pleasure.

Barbiturates are highly addictive, which is one reason why they are rarely prescribed nowadays. For a list of brand names, see Appendix 1.

How they are used

1. *Swallowed*.

2. *Injected*.

Health risks

1. *Overdose*. The line between taking enough pills to get the desired effect and overdosing is a thin one. Only a few extra pills can cause death. Barbiturates can also be lethal when combined with alcohol.

2. *Injecting* with barbiturates is extremely dangerous because the powder does not dissolve properly, causing abscesses.

Patent medicines and analgesics

A wide variety of drugs is sold over the counter without a doctor's prescription. Used as directed, these are safe and effective. But addicts sometimes use these drugs in excessive quantities. Should the tablets contain a small amount of opiate drugs among other ingredients, they give, if not pleasure, then the relief from painful reality which the addict is seeking.

Cough mixtures, diarrhoea mixtures, and painkillers can all be used in this way by addicts. Codeine linctus, and kaolin and morphine mixture are some of those commonly used. They are not often the first choice of addicts, but are used when the favourite drug cannot be obtained.

Health risks

Overdose. Over-the-counter medicines and pills contain only a small amount of opiates, and therefore the addict needs to take large quantities to get the desired effect. However, there is often a mixture of drugs in patent medicines, which means that the other ingredients, like paracetamol, may be dangerous in overdose.

Alcohol

The chemical name for alcohol is ethyl alcohol. Mixed with water in varying proportions, it is found in spirits, wine and beer. It is part of the social tradition of many countries.

After drinking, alcohol is absorbed into the bloodstream and its effect lasts up to several hours. In most people it produces feelings of relaxation and pleasure.

Alcohol is addictive for some people, though it is not as addictive as heroin. Doctors tend to call these people alcoholics rather than 'ethyl alcohol addicts', though the latter is just as good a description. It is the mood-altering effect of ethyl alcohol in drinks – whether in beer, cider and spirits or in a bottle of vintage wine – which alcoholics seek.

How often

Alcoholics may be daily drinkers, drinking round the clock from morning to night. Or they may start drinking only in the evening. As the alcohol stays in the bloodstream for many hours, the alcoholic can go for quite some time between drinks. It takes the body about an hour to process one ounce of alcohol.

Some alcoholics have a discontinuous pattern of 'binge drinking'. They may be sober for days, weeks or even months, and then go off on a drinking spree.

Health risks

1. *Lifestyle*. In the later stages of the illness, alcoholics forget to eat and do not look after themselves. Accidents are also common. Crime, violence and sometimes prostitution occur among alcoholics.

2. *Ulcers, liver disease, heart trouble, circulatory disease and brain damage* are some of the results of alcoholic drinking.

3. *Depression, paranoia and memory impairment* are among the mental effects of the illness.

4. *Overdose*. Overdosing on alcohol alone is rare, but accidental overdoses from a combination of drink and drugs are not uncommon – as hospital casualty departments at weekends know only too well.

Other drugs

There are other drugs that can cause dependence. Anaesthetists and dentists occasionally become addicted to laughing gas, or other gases. In the United States, the so-called 'designer drugs', including one with the inappropriate name of 'Ecstasy', are fairly common on the streets. Amyl nitrate – or 'poppers', sometimes used as an extra during sex – is also widely available but not commonly used continuously.

Some addicts will try literally anything. 'I would take whatever was offered,' admits one recovering addict. 'If I was feeling cautious, I would ask what it was first. But I wasn't usually feeling cautious.'

Women and drugs

Women who become addicted to drugs and drink face special dangers. Neither drugs nor drink are safe for pregnant women. They may affect the development of the baby within the womb, even in the first few weeks after conception. Indeed, even before conception, drug-using can affect the health of the mother-to-be, since most addicts have a lifestyle characterised by poor nutrition.

Drugs or drink may cause withdrawal problems for the newly born baby too. They may also pass through the mother's body into the breast milk, which can cause a further problem.

The exact dangers of either drugs or drink in pregnancy are not yet fully known. Research is still going on.

Heroin

Heroin addicts have a higher number of stillborn babies. They also give birth to babies who are smaller in size than ordinary babies. When they are born, such children have to go through heroin withdrawal in the first days of their life. Generally they are less healthy, and seem less alert. Restlessness, agitation and more frequent crying have been reported. Their poor start may affect them for their first year.

Methadone

Babies born to methadone-addicted mothers are not as small as those born to heroin addicts, but they suffer withdrawal symptoms which may be more prolonged than those affecting heroin addicts' babies. In general they have as bad a start in life – or even a worse one – as the babies of heroin-addicted mothers.

Cannabis

Some research suggests that cannabis may cause birth defects and a lower birth weight for babies in the womb. Babies may have the facial appearance that goes with the 'foetal alcohol syndrome' – flattened face, short upturned nose and slanting eyes. It is possible, however, that this is caused by the fact that cannabis-addicted mothers may be drinking heavily as well.

Tranquillisers and sleeping pills

These may cause birth defects in the early stages of pregnancy. If their mothers have been taking tranquillisers, newly born babies are sometimes drowsy, displaying the 'floppy-baby syndrome'.

The babies of tranquilliser-addicted mothers may have to go through the painful withdrawal process. Their withdrawals are much more prolonged than their mothers'.

Barbiturates

Some research suggests barbiturates produce birth defects in unborn babies. These drugs cause painful withdrawal reactions in the newly born babies of barbiturate-addicted mothers.

Alcohol

Alcohol can cause birth defects, including brain damage, to babies in the womb. It also slows down the growth of the foetus. There is strong evidence to suggest that even medium to heavy drinking, let alone alcoholic drinking, can cause reduced birth weights and brain mass in otherwise normal babies. A recognisable 'foetal alcohol syndrome' is found in newly born babies, who have a flattened face, slanting eyes and upturned nose.

Withdrawal effects have been seen in the newly born babies of alcoholic mothers. These babies have tremors, sometimes even seizures, in the first few days of life.

Other drugs

There are reports of birth defects among babies whose mothers have taken LSD, PCP and amphetamines, but research is still fragmentary. Withdrawal effects from amphetamines and PCP have also been detected in the newly born. Little is known about the effects of cocaine upon the unborn or the newly born child. The other opiate drugs, like codeine, can cause withdrawal in newly born infants.

Despite the lack of research, it is now abundantly clear that babies born to addicted mothers are at risk. Drug addicts who become pregnant should seek medical advice as early as possible. Abrupt withdrawal from drugs, or fluctuations in the amount taken, may harm the unborn baby. The pregnant addict should *always* get expert medical advice about her drug-taking, whether she is thinking of stopping using drugs or intending to continue. Medical advice and supervision from a doctor specialising in treating pregnant addicts is essential.

3
How Family and Friends Can Intervene

If there is somebody in your family who you suspect may be taking drugs or drinking too much, you probably feel extremely anxious about it. Parents in particular are often utterly terrified by the thought that their children may be taking drugs or sniffing glue. Their fear comes partly from their ignorance of one undoubted fact – chemical dependence is an illness which can be and *is* treated successfully.

Do not panic or lose hope. Ignore the hysteria in the newspaper headlines. Put old wives' tales out of your head. Take no notice of the warnings and advice which come from people who know nothing about drug dependence.

Drug addiction is an illness like any other. It can be treated by experts who understand it. Drug addicts and alcoholics do get well and go on to lead happy and useful lives. The stories in Chapter 1 show this.

Moreover, families can indirectly help addicts recover. The way the family deals with the ill person in their midst can *increase their chances of recovery*. Your actions and reactions will make a huge difference – if you make the effort to understand what these should be.

This chapter is addressed to parents, but the principles also apply to brothers, sisters, partners and friends. Later in the chapter there will be some special words for those readers who are not parents.

Tell-tale signs of chemical dependence

One major problem faces the families of drug addicts or alcoholics – their own unwillingness to believe the worst. Nobody wants to admit that their child or their partner may be addicted to drugs or alcohol; therefore they may unconsciously try to avoid facing the truth.

Here are some of the signs by which the family can tell what is really going on.

Behaviour

Addicts and alcoholics begin to show sudden and inappropriate mood swings while they are under the influence of either drugs or alcohol. They may be obviously high at an inappropriate time, or they may be utterly depressed for no good reason.

There is also often a lack of concentration and an impaired memory. Those who are using cannabis can become extremely apathetic.

Appearance

Drug addicts often lose weight and develop a fragile look. Pupils may be enormous (amphetamines and cocaine) or abnormally small (opiates). Those who are snorting drugs may have a permanently sniffing nose. A general sleepiness alternates with sudden snapping awake. Addicts who inject will show scars known as 'track marks' where they have put in the needle – or they will wear long-sleeved clothes to hide these even in the height of summer. Addicts may spend a lot of time rubbing their noses (if they have been snorting) or yawning and perspiring. Sleeplessness might be due to amphetamines and cocaine.

Alcoholics are often flushed and sweaty. You can smell drink on their breath, or even smell the alcohol coming out of their pores. Alcoholics in the early stages, however, may show none of these signs.

Sense of time

Addicts begin to lose their sense of time. They spend the day in bed, the night out. Alcoholics have memory blanks, when they have no idea at all of what happened or what they did, even though they appeared to be functioning normally.

Suspicious objects

These include lemons or citric-acid packets; small paper envelopes in which the drug was sold; cigarette papers for smoking cannabis; silver foil; syringes and needles; hidden bottles (empty or full) of alcoholic drinks. You may also notice a sudden drop in your own wine or spirits supply, or find that bottles have been watered down.

Loss of interests

As the illness progresses, addicts and alcoholics lose interest in outside things. Activities they once enjoyed now mean nothing to them. Friends who do not use drugs or drink drop away. Addicts withdraw from family life. Alcoholics show a kind of mental obsession with drink and drinking occasions, and a dissatisfaction with work, work colleagues and family.

Ethical deterioration

As the addiction gets worse, the addict becomes secretive, tells lies, steals money, behaves in a way which is entirely out of character for the person he or she was *before* drugs or drink. Dr Jekyll becomes Mr Hyde, sometimes in front of the family's very eyes.

It is important to realise that addicts, like ordinary people, differ. Some addicts show all these signs very quickly indeed and cannot conceal the problem from the family. In others, the addiction progresses more slowly and it may be a very long time before the family realises what is going on.

Some addicts and alcoholics manage to function quite well in society, despite their illness. Company directors and television producers can be alcoholics, as well as meths drinkers in the gutter. In the same way, not all addicts are living in filthy squats. They may be holding down good jobs and have all the trappings of success – yet be dependent on drugs or drink. A questionnaire in Chapter 4 gives some insight into addiction.

How the family reacts

Most parents react with fear, despair, guilt and anger at the realisation that their child is on drugs. The sheer pain they feel is almost indescribable. It is usually followed by a terrible sense of impotent rage and fury.

Mothers especially feel guilt. They ask themselves: 'What did I do wrong to cause this?' They are ashamed to let anybody outside the family know about it.

The drug-using addict will happily prey on this guilt. It's like the reverse of the possessive-mother syndrome. The child emotionally blackmails the parent in order to get his own way.

'My parents wanted to help me, to keep me out of trouble,' recalls Nick, a recovering addict. 'I went to great lengths to make them feel responsible for my addiction. My disease robbed me of the ability to demonstrate love.

'My parents stopped seeing friends because they were embarrassed by my behaviour. They were terrified. They wanted to know everything I was doing. They were always nagging and checking up on me. I just thought of them as a hindrance.'

The next stage in the family's reaction is usually to start a desperate search for a way to 'cure' their addict. They try to get the help of doctors, family friends who may talk to the addict, drug-dependence clinics, teachers, or the addict's old friends from the days before he started using drugs.

Susanna's story

Susanna is a well-dressed woman in her forties who works in an auctioneering firm. She separated from her husband some years ago, and has two boys. The first sign that something was wrong came when her younger son, Ian, then eighteen years old and at a public school, got into trouble for smoking cannabis.

That summer, Ian left school and went to a summer course in France. When he came back, Susanna began to realise that something was wrong. Somehow Ian's attitude was different. He was aggressive, difficult to live with, and dirty.

'I was frantically worried from then on,' recalls Susanna. 'I asked advice from a friend who had run an addiction unit. Ian went to see him and conned him into believing it was only pot. The friend said that what Ian needed was a more exciting life!'

When Ian caught hepatitis, Susanna began to realise that her son was on heroin. 'What had crept up was the stealing. I would think "I'm sure I had a fiver in my purse. Oh well, perhaps I didn't." '

She took him to a doctor for his hepatitis, then took him home to convalesce. And when Ian ran away from home, she chased him round various squats. 'I used to put notes through the door saying "I'm always here if you need me. Mummy loves you." '

Susanna asked various doctors for help. They told her that Ian would have to go to a drug-dependence unit. She went to her GP, who simply said: 'You must persuade him to have treatment in the unit at the local hospital.'

'But there was no way I could persuade him. He came back for two days, then left home again. I followed him surreptitiously in a taxi to see where he was going and wrote down the address.'

The next thing that happened was that Ian was had up in court for fraud. He'd forged a signature on a cheque. Susanna hired a solicitor for him, and he got off with a £500 fine. She paid it because 'it seemed better than prison.'

Ian then promised her he would stop using drugs. He got a job and started living at home again. 'I thought that maybe living at home with a good evening meal and going to bed early would work the miracle. I had it all mapped out for him, that I would find him a flat with some nice people in it.'

It didn't last. Three weeks later, Ian went back to using drugs. All Susanna's efforts had been useless.

Trying to control the addict using drugs is a waste of time.
YOU CANNOT CONTROL AN ADDICT OR AN ALCOHOLIC

Here are some of the things people have done in vain attempts to stop an addict using drugs or an alcoholic drinking:

1. They have asked the addict to promise not to use drugs any more. The addict has promised – and gone back to using drugs. In just the same way families often ask their alcoholic to swear off drink. He does so – only to go back to drinking.

2. They have thrown away the addict's drug supply or emptied the alcoholic's bottles. The addict has gone out to buy new drugs and the alcoholic has gone out and bought more drink.

3. They have wept, they have threatened, they have coaxed, they have bribed, and they have nagged. The addict has continued to use drugs. The alcoholic has continued to drink.

4. They have asked the family doctor, or the minister, or a friend, or a social worker 'to have a serious talk' with the sick person. The addict has gone on using drugs and the alcoholic has gone on drinking.

There are thousands more schemes, dodges, tricks and other

devices that the family tried in growing desperation. Some of them may result in the addict or alcoholic stopping using drink and drugs for a few days or weeks. But in the long run they do not work. They do not work because of one simple fact:

The addict will only stop using drugs when he or she wants to stop – or when somebody makes drug-using so uncomfortable that he or she has to ask for help.

What makes an addict decide to stop?

Let's pause here and consider why addicts decide to stop using drugs and get well. Such a decision isn't an easy one for them. Addicts fear withdrawal and they cannot conceive of a life without drugs. So why do they stop taking drugs?

They stop because in their own minds going on using drugs seems even more painful than stopping.

Putting it another way – addicts decide to stop using drugs when the consequences of their drug-use get too painful.

For some addicts the consequence of drug-using which makes them stop is something serious, like a prison sentence. For some it's the moment when they are chucked out of the family home. For some it may be a realisation that nobody is going to rescue them any more. Families can raise the level of pain when they withdraw support and stop picking up the pieces.

Nick remembers what finally brought him to the realisation that he must stop using drugs. 'My parents eventually couldn't take any more. They told me: "We love you, but seeing you is doing us no good." They asked me to stop coming home. I was astounded. How on earth could this happen? About three weeks after that I went into a treatment centre, and then joined Narcotics Anonymous. I have been clean and sober since.'

So the message for parents is clear. Addicts stop using drugs when the painful consequences of their drug-use get too much to bear. If this is so, parents must let them *experience* those consequences.

Stop helping the addict stay ill

Most ill people need tender loving care to nurse them back to health. Drug addicts and alcoholics don't. Chemical dependence is an illness in which kindness can literally kill the sick person.

Most parents try to cure their addicts or alcoholics by 'helping' them. They find them flats, get them new jobs, pay the fines, get them proper legal help, take them to doctors, buy them new clothes, take them to psychiatrists for their supposed 'underlying problems', and a thousand other futile solutions.

Addicts usually co-operate enthusiastically. They promise that of course they will stop using drugs and that it will all be different if only they have the new flat, new job, new clothes, don't have to go to prison, don't see a doctor, or if they have their doubtful underlying Freudian problems sorted out.

Sometimes they manage a few weeks, occasionally a few months, without drugs. Then they go back on them again.

All this 'helping' allows the addict to escape the consequences of drug-using. *It helps the addict or the alcoholic stay ill.*

Let the addict suffer the consequences

Parents *can* do something that will really help their child come closer to recovery: they can let the addict or the alcoholic suffer the consequences of drug-using or drinking. This is what those who treat addicts call 'intervention' or 'tough love'.

Susanna discovered the secret of this technique just after Ian's first court case. She joined Families Anonymous, the self-help organisation like Narcotics Anonymous, which helps and advises the families and friends of addicts.

'I found this amazing atmosphere and kindness from others who were in the same situation,' she recalls. 'I also found that I had been doing it all wrong. By rushing round London after Ian, I was giving him the feeling that he could use me.'

For several months she saw almost nothing of Ian. She stopped trying to find out where he was living. She began to get on with her own life. She also started taking more notice of her elder son, whom she had almost ignored at the height of her obsession with Ian. He had felt shut out from his mother's love.

Then, one Tuesday, she had a phone call from a London magistrates' court. 'Ian rang me to say he was in trouble again. He'd been shoplifting. He'd got to produce another fine or go to prison.

'I had to take a deep breath and pause. If I hadn't been to Families Anonymous I'd have been over at that court with my cheque book in my hand. But this time I knew I shouldn't. I felt it was rather like that moment when you take a little boy to school and let him go in the playground for the first time. I said to Ian down the phone: "I'm not going to pay the fine for you." '

Ian went to prison. While he was there, Susanna visited him and he told her he wanted to stop using drugs. When he came out, he managed to stay off drugs for two weeks, then got a place in a residential treatment centre. Since then he has stayed clean in Narcotics Anonymous.

Letting Ian experience the consequences of his using was what helped him towards recovery.

Intervening to make the addict seek help

It is very unusual for addicts or alcoholics to seek help unless there is no other alternative. The people most able to force them to look at their drug or drink problem are family, friends or employers.

The inability of alcoholics or addicts even to recognise that they need help is called 'denial'. To put it simply, denial is an attitude that 'My drinking or drug-taking is not really that bad!'

In fact, those around them can see that their behaviour is obviously progressively more disastrous. The solution is to use a crisis that the drinking or drug-taking has created, so that they have no alternative but to seek help. This is called intervention and it is best done in a caring but firm manner. Here are three examples of intervention.

1. After a crisis, a wife may say to her husband: 'I love you, Michael, but unless you do something about your drinking, I am going to see a solicitor. If you accept treatment, though, I'll support you all the way.'

2. After a crisis with her addicted daughter, a mother may say: 'Unless you get help with your addiction, you will have to leave home. Go to Narcotics Anonymous or get into treatment.'

3. At work, the boss or the personnel manager can have the alcoholic in and relate the history of his deterioration in job performance. 'Tom, you were once a valued and trusted employee,' he may say. 'I know you can be that again *if* you seek help for your drinking problem. Otherwise we can't keep you. You have had numerous warnings and this is the last.'

In each case there must be a commitment to follow through. If the alcoholic or addict does not get help, then the wife must see the solicitor, the mother must make her daughter leave home and the personnel manager must dismiss the employee. Otherwise the options become meaningless.

It must be made clear that abstinence is the expected goal, and that a change to more responsible behaviour must also occur through treatment or through involvement in the self-help groups of Narcotics Anonymous or Alcoholics Anonymous.

In our experience, despite the fact that the alcoholic or addict is *forced* to seek help, the outcome is usually successful. It is common to hear later from the recovering person: 'If only someone had forced me to face this years ago, I wouldn't have wasted so much of my life or hurt so many people.'

One of the most tragic aspects of this illness is that the drinking alcoholic or drug-using addict will only grudgingly accept help when there is no other choice.

Letting the addict know how you feel

Many families do not face such stark decisions. If their addict is on cannabis, dependent on prescribed drugs or on alcohol, the illness may be more subtle. On the outside, the addict or alcoholic may be functioning fairly well, keeping down a job and apparently not much harmed by the illness.

The chances are that the illness first shows itself at home, among the family. While in the outside world, the addict or alcoholic seems to behave acceptably; the brunt of his bad behaviour is borne by those he or she lives with. He's a street angel and a home devil.

We have said that nagging, coaxing, threatening and bullying the addict or alcoholic is a waste of time. But that doesn't mean you should stay silent like some suffering Patient Griselda. Far from it. Let the addict or alcoholic know how you feel. Tell him or her clearly and directly when you are upset or hurt or angry.

Shouting or crying or losing your temper will simply mean the message isn't heard. Tell it like it is, in a caring way. Say: 'I was angry last night when you came back drunk/stoned and smashed up the television set.'

Say how you feel when the addict or the alcoholic can hear it, when he is not stoned or drunk – perhaps the morning after. Say it in a firm but caring voice. And say it just once. When you have said it, carry on with what you were doing. Otherwise you'll be tempted to elaborate, argue or even draw back, start apologising yourself, and end up being manipulated again!

This technique achieves two things:

1. It confronts the addict or the alcoholic with the consequences of getting stoned or drunk. Remember he may literally not know

what he has done – especially if he has been suffering from alcoholic amnesia. This way, you tell him.

2. It allows you to express your feelings, and shows the addict that you cannot just be used or abused at will.

3. It stops an argument developing. Addicts and alcoholics are masters at twisting words to suit them. A good argument allows them to put you in the wrong and to ignore the fact that their behaviour started it.

Tough love

The relatives of addicts call this tough love. Tough love means stopping trying to rescue the addict, and starting to let him suffer. Because only by suffering the painful consequences of chemical dependence will the addict begin to realise he has the problem.

It's just like the tough love you have to practise with a young child. If you say that a seven-year-old should be in bed by eight o'clock, the child may well try to coax you to change your mind. Then he'll try sulking or temper tantrums. If you back down and let him stay up, you are in danger of bringing up a spoilt child. He learns by experience that although you say one thing, you actually practise another. Your actions don't back up your words, so he stops listening to your words.

It's just the same with the addict. Practising tough love doesn't always come easily. Many parents are so frantic with anxiety that they simply won't pause to listen to advice. They go on trying to control their addict.

They say that they want their addict to stop using drugs. But their actions show just the opposite. Through their actions they actually reward him for using – by finding accommodation, fixing jobs, paying fines and in general giving him all their attention. Some misguided parents even buy drugs for their addicts – in this way literally helping the addict stay on drugs.

What drug dependence does to the addict's family

Gillian was a rich woman with two daughters, Jenny and Isabel. Jenny started using drugs just after leaving school. Her mother tried everything to 'help' her. She found her a place in college, and then another one when Jenny got chucked out for using drugs. She found her new places to live so that she wouldn't have to meet her old drug-using friends. She bought her a new wardrobe to help her morale. She found her doctors, and more doctors, and yet more doctors. These prescribed drugs. Jenny just abused them.

The rest of the family looked on with mounting horror as Gillian seemed to get more and more obsessed with the drug problem. Her other daughter, Isabel, became very upset indeed. Her mother more or less ignored her. It was as if she would only get attention if *she* started using drugs herself.

Whatever Gillian did, Jenny went on using drugs. She'd make promises, and then she'd go back to drugs. Gillian got more and more frantic. She decided that it was all her fault. Finally, feeling a complete failure, she committed suicide.

Chemical dependence had wrecked the whole family. Jenny the drug user was still taking drugs. Her mother had killed herself. Her sister had lost, first of all, her mother's love and attention, then finally her mother herself.

Most families see what drug dependence is doing to the addict. What they can't see is *what drug dependence is doing to them*.

The family is emotionally damaged by the illness

When somebody is taking drugs or drink, it doesn't affect just them. It affects the whole family and any intimate friends around them. The addict's sick behaviour causes waves of emotional damage to those that love them.

For every drug-using addict or drinking alcoholic, there are four other family members whose lives are adversely affected. Chemical dependence distorts family life so badly that the family itself starts going downhill.

Family members often start isolating themselves from a normal social life because they are embarrassed by the fact that they have a drug addict in their midst. They may stop taking proper rest and recreation. 'I feel guilty having a nice time when I know my child is out there suffering,' is their response. This makes the situation even worse.

1. *The family suffers more than the addict.* Addicts or alcoholics avoid emotional pain by simply getting stoned or drunk. They don't feel the emotional turmoil that is going on around them.

2. *Addicts and alcoholics may actually thrive in such circumstances.* If other members of the family are behaving in an inappropriate way, their own sick behaviour doesn't show up so much. They need not face their own destructive behaviour, because they can point to the distorted behaviour of everybody else instead. It gives

them an excellent excuse to go on using drugs and drink.

3. *If family members get too emotionally damaged, they won't be there when they are needed* – at that moment when the addict or alcoholic decides that perhaps he wants to do something about his drug-using or drinking.

Get on with your own life

Families who have an addict or alcoholic need to stop giving all their attention to the drug user or the drinker. Making the sick person the focus of attention is extremely bad for him. It encourages him to manipulate those around him.

Start practising emotional detachment. If the addict is angry or unhappy, it doesn't mean you have to have the same feelings. Don't let the emotional disorder of the addict's life spill over into yours.

Start focusing on your own life. Take proper rest. Take proper recreation. Go to the cinema, the theatre, parties, the pub and so forth, just as you would do if everything were all right.

Even partners of alcoholics or addicts, who may be in financially very difficult circumstances, can do something they enjoy – even if it's only going to a museum, taking a walk in the park, or watching a favourite soap opera on television.

What's good for you is good for the alcoholic or the addict.

Make a conscious effort to rebuild your own life. Repair your social life. You may well not want to share this with the addict or the alcoholic, since drug users and alcoholics are not fun to have around. Make your own friends.

Join Families Anonymous or Al-anon. In these meetings you will receive all the love and encouragement you need from people who have been in similar circumstances. The phone numbers you need are in Appendix 2. These self-help organisations are made up of families and friends who know what it is like to have an addict or an alcoholic in their life. There are mothers, fathers, wives, husbands, partners, lovers, sisters, brothers and just friends. They *know* what you are going through.

To a newcomer, full of guilt and anger and despair, the meetings may seem rather strange at first. That is why it is very important to go to at least six of their meetings before making up your mind whether to let them help you.

Clean your side of the street

Most family members have been so busy worrying about the addict or the alcoholic that they haven't paid much attention to what else is going on around them. And sometimes there are other problems of chemical dependence which have stayed hidden.

After all, when the full drama of 'Rescuing the Junkie' is being played out by the family, more subtle forms of addiction go unnoticed. The family member who is dependent on prescribed drugs like tranquillisers and sleeping pills doesn't get up to the outrageous actions of the junkie, but she or he is just as sick. So is the alcoholic drinker, even if he or she 'scores' alcohol quite legally from the off-licence or pub. If you think you too might have a problem with your drinking or with prescribed drugs, the questionnaire in the next chapter may help you as well as your addict.

It is a fact that more than one in four drug addicts come from homes where there is already an addiction problem – usually to alcohol or prescribed drugs. Sometimes this problem skips a generation, having occurred further back with grandparents.

Addicts rather like this situation. It allows them to play the guilt game with their parents. 'Your drinking made me into a junkie', is their cry. If you clean up your own act, it takes the wind out of their sails.

Partners, wives and husbands

If you are married to, or in a committed relationship with an addict or an alcoholic, you may be not just emotionally damaged but also damaged financially, and sometimes literally beaten. Battered wives and partners often come from alcoholic marriages.

Wives, in particular, tend to get emotionally distressed. They are often financially dependent on their husbands. They are struggling to bring up children in a home that is warped by alcohol or drugs. *Quite often they do not realise how bad the situation has become.*

Dominating alcoholics or addicts can often persuade partners either that it is all their fault or that they are the ones who are mad. Partners even get blamed for the children's normal growing-up pains. Things go from bad to worse in the home, without the partner realising the full seriousness of the illness.

It is vital to start getting help from Al-anon or Families

Anonymous *before the position gets too bad*. Only in that way can you help yourself, your children and (whatever they may say about it) your partner.

Sisters and brothers

Sadly, addicts have been known to recruit their brothers and sisters into drug-using. Most addicts prefer to get stoned in company, and they will therefore try to get others into drug-using.

The other problem faced by brothers and sisters is that they get little or no attention from their parents. While the pointless search is on to 'cure' the addict, they may be quite neglected.

It is therefore extremely important that you should get help for yourselves from Families Anonymous – no matter what your parents are doing. You will find other young people there who have gone through the experience of seeing a sister or a brother become addicted. Teenagers with alcoholic brothers, sisters or parents can join Alateen, which is part of the Al-anon organisation.

Just like parents of addicts, brothers and sisters should make sure they get on with their own lives. Don't let your schoolwork or career suffer. Make sure you have an enjoyable social life, and an enjoyable love life too.

Making yourself suffer won't help the addict. Remember: *what's good for you is good for the addict.*

Checklist for family intervention

Many of the ideas we've put forward in this chapter may seem strange to you. But the principles do work. If you follow the suggestions you will minimise the damage that chemical dependence wreaks on those around the addict, and you will give your addict a better chance of getting well.

Here's what to do:

1. Join Families Anonymous or Al-anon. Get support and encouragement from others in your position.

2. Stop blaming yourself. You didn't cause the addict to get addicted. Take no notice when the addict or alcoholic blames you. He would, wouldn't he? That way he can have an excuse to go on using or drinking.

3. Stop trying to rescue the addict or alcoholic. You can't control his addiction, and you can't cure it either. Visiting the addict in some filthy squat just to check he is still alive simply punishes *you*. It does not keep the addict alive. Rescue efforts are wasted efforts.

4. Stop trying to understand the addict or the alcoholic. It's a waste of thinking time. Pondering the underlying reasons why someone becomes an addict or an alcoholic wastes energy and gets nowhere. Even the experts disagree on this one. Stop asking the unanswerable 'Why?' and start focusing on treatment.

5. Stop threatening, nagging, coaxing, bullying, bribing, preaching or lecturing. Instead of all this, you can start letting the addict or alcoholic know how you feel in a caring way.

6. Let the addict or alcoholic suffer the consequences of his own drug-using or drinking. That means letting him or her go downhill. But only by standing back in this way is there any chance that your addict will want to stop.

7. Start offering the addict or alcoholic choices. 'If you want help, we'll help you. If you want to stay sick, you are on your own.'

8. Get on with your own life. Look after your own needs and desires. Do things to make yourself happy. *What's good for you is good for the addict*.

9. Start rebuilding family life. Remember that you have healthy children who need your time and love. Minimise the damage to yourself and the rest of the family.

10. Learn about the disease. Once you do so, you can stop all that fretting about which drugs, how much, or how often. You can also stop listening to all that well-meaning advice from the ignorant, who sometimes include journalists, TV personalities and, alas, even some well-intentioned doctors and social workers who have been conned by addicts and alcoholics.

PART THREE

For the Addict and the Alcoholic

4

Chemical Dependence: Are You an Addict or an Alcoholic?

Since drugs are so obviously harmful to people, why on earth do addicts go on taking them? Outsiders are usually baffled by the persistence with which addicts and alcoholics will go on taking drugs and drinking – no matter how often they are warned, lectured, threatened, coaxed, helped and even 'treated'.

This persistence is at the heart of the illness which affects addicts and alcoholics – the illness of chemical dependence.

Addicts and alcoholics are not bad people, no matter how bad their behaviour sometimes gets. They are ill people. For chemical dependence is an illness of the body and mind, most of all an illness of the emotions, either deadening or exaggerating feelings.

After all, what sane person would go on taking heroin knowing what it is doing to him? What sane person would take tranquillisers for years at a time? What sane person would continue drinking, when it is obviously doing him harm?

Denial

'I used to tell myself I wasn't addicted to the stuff, even while I was putting the needle in to inject,' says Roger. 'I could handle it. I could give it up any time.'

Here is the mystery of chemical dependence. Addicts or alcoholics are often literally the last people to see what the illness is doing to them. If they do see, they are blind to the obvious way to recover. This is the mental side of the illness.

It is an illness which tells the sufferer that he hasn't got it.

An addict or an alcoholic is characterised by denial. He or she is unable or unwilling to admit to the problem.

There is a third aspect to the illness of chemical dependence. This is the ethical degradation, what recovering addicts sometimes call the 'spiritual' side of the illness. An addict's behaviour becomes worse and worse as the illness progresses.

Addicts and alcoholics behave badly because they use drugs and drink: they are sick and therefore their behaviour deteriorates. It is not that they are bad people: their bad behaviour is usually the outward symptom of their inner illness of chemical dependence.

How to recognise chemical dependence

Addicts and alcoholics show definite signs of their chemical dependence. Here are some of the symptoms.

Lack of control

They cannot control their drug-taking or drinking. This means that they are unable to predict with any certainty what will happen after the first drug or drink. There is a random compulsiveness about their behaviour.

The drug is controlling them, rather than they controlling the drug. In the early stages of the illness there may be some control left. For a few days or weeks, the addict seems to have it licked. He is not out of control. But eventually the control slips. This applies to alcoholics as much as to drug users.

In the long run, addicts cannot consistently reduce the amount they take, or regulate it as they would wish. They may fully intend to stop taking drugs, yet be unable to do so. Or they may intend to reduce the amount they take, and yet not be able to manage it. In the same way, their behaviour becomes more and more unpredictable once the drug is taken.

At later stages there is much less control. An addict may be unable to be in a house where there are drugs without finishing them – even if he knows that he needs to save some for the next day.

'It was a downhill struggle. I used to go for a few days without drugs. Then that would justify me thinking I wasn't an addict, so I could reward myself by taking them again,' recalls Tracey, a recovering addict now in her twenties with a job and a new life. 'I was unable to stop. I tried doctors, psychiatrists, acupuncturists. I'd get detoxed. Then when I'd been off it a week or so, I felt so bad I went back on. It was a vicious circle for about five years.'

Surreptitious behaviour

Addicts tend to be devious about their drug habit. They will lie repeatedly, even idiotically, to those around them. They will hide their drug gear. They will disappear into the lavatory for a fix, hoping nobody will realise what they are doing. Finding hiding places for the drugs is another obsession. Many addicts will have several hiding places. They may hide their drugs even though they live alone.

This surreptitious behaviour is seen in alcoholics too. They lie about how much they drink. They start hiding bottles. Or they drink in pubs where they are not known. They visit different supermarkets and off-licences to buy their bottles in the hope that nobody will know what they are doing.

Both addicts and alcoholics will surround themselves with those who condone their drug-using or drinking. There is nothing they like better than being able to point the finger at others whose habit is even worse than their own. This is the equivalent of hiding a needle in a haystack, since it hides the full extent of their own drink or drugs problem.

And this surreptitious behaviour is often accompanied by great shame, guilt and fear. Women alcoholics in particular suffer from anguish about their drinking.

Mental obsession

The drug takes over the addict's mind. Life begins to centre round drug-taking. Much effort is put into ensuring a supply. Addicts tend to drift into the society of other addicts. Their talk is all about drugs. Alcoholics may show an obsession with drink, talking endlessly about how much was drunk, by whom, and where.

To the outsider, the addict's world is an intensely boring one. Hobbies, interests and friendships have all slipped away.

'I told my best friend that I was emigrating to Australia,' recalls James. 'I just didn't want to see him. I used just to stay in my room and fix.'

Addiction, dependence and chemicals

The old word for this sickness was 'drug addiction'. Because it is used by so many people in ordinary life, we sometimes use it in this book. But today many doctors talk about 'drug dependence'. When we are anxious to be strictly accurate, we use the term 'chemical dependence' – for a good reason: the illness applies to all chemicals, drugs and drink alike.

Heroin addicts, tranquilliser addicts and alcoholics all have the same sickness. They are dependent on chemicals. These chemicals can be heroin or cocaine, tranquillisers or sleeping pills, or the ethyl alcohol found in a bottle.

And to an addict, the exact chemical does not matter. Of course, all addicts have their drug of choice. A heroin addict prefers heroin. But if he or she can't get any, cocaine or methadone or tranquillisers or alcohol will do at a pinch.

It's like visiting an ice-cream parlour. You go into an ice-cream parlour wanting some chocolate-chip ice-cream. If the chocolate-chip ice-cream has run out, you won't go out empty-handed. You'll settle for butterscotch, strawberry or even plain vanilla. Just as long as it's ice-cream. Addicts feel just the same way about drugs. 'If you're not near the drug you love, you'll love the drug you're near,' is a familiar saying among recovering addicts.

And this includes alcohol. Addicts who have given up drugs often turn to alcohol and rapidly find they are alcoholics. Ricky's story in Chapter 1 shows how this happens. In the same way, alcoholics off the booze often find they've become addicted to tranquillisers in place of drink. There will be more about this in our chapters on recovery.

For practical purposes, drug addiction and alcoholism are the same thing. Alcoholics are just ethyl-alcohol addicts under a different name and they are drinking a legally available drug. The illness they have in common with drug addicts is the illness of chemical dependence.

That's why there is only one answer to chemical dependence – complete abstinence from any kind of mood-altering drug. No heroin, no cocaine, no tranquillisers and no alcohol.

The need to change

Addicts also have to change themselves. They need to change their feelings, their attitudes and their lifestyle. This inward and outward change is what protects them against going back on drugs. It sounds tough. But this is a killer disease, and half measures get you nowhere. You don't even get half well from half measures. You stay wholly ill.

The golden rule about recovering from chemical dependence is that half measures don't work.

In the long run, offering an easy answer for chemical dependence is not being kind to addicts. Some people treat addicts by giving them legally prescribed drugs in the place of illegal drugs because they think this is kinder.

It isn't. Take the example of Mary, a young addict who was trying to get off heroin. The doctor treating her gave her prescriptions for DF 118 (dihydrocodeine tartrate) and tranquillisers. For weeks at a time she took these pills instead of illegal drugs. And that way she did not learn to live without drugs. Eventually, weeks later, she had to be weaned off the prescription drugs, and suffered the much more painful withdrawals that occur after tranquilliser dependence. Her recovery was delayed and made more painful.

The only kindness to a suffering addict is to help them get properly well, not to enable them to stay sick.

Recognising your addiction

So what if you are somebody who takes drugs?

It's not what kind of drug you are taking that matters. It's not how much of that drug. It's what that drug is doing to you and others.

If you are a drug addict, that drug will be causing problems in your life.

For some people these problems will be serious ones – court appearances, prison sentences, hospital treatment, overdoses, suicide attempts, prostitution, crime. For others the problems are far less obvious. But they are there. The addict seems to be functioning all right on the surface but there are the tell-tale signs – lost jobs, warnings at work, absences from work, physical sickness like abscesses and withdrawal symptoms when trying to cut down, the necessity to fit life round a pattern of drug-using or drinking.

Often the first signs of trouble are in the family. Addicts will probably find they are faced with nagging wives, furious husbands, unhappy children, frantic parents. There may be violence in the home. And old friends – friends from the days before the drug took over – are dropping away.

For chemical dependence is an illness which sometimes starts quietly. Some people experiment with heroin and deteriorate rapidly to overdoses, squats, crime and violence. In others the illness creeps up quietly. Slowly drugs and alcohol tighten their grip on the person's life. At first, the addict seems to be able to control the drug.

At this point, the addict probably blames those around him for his troubles. His family, who are making all that fuss about drugs, simply don't understand. It's their fault in the first place that he got ill. They just don't understand.

It gets worse

Yet chemical dependence is a progressive illness. It gets worse every day, week and month that the addict continues using drugs.

'For a time it was fun. I tried lots of different drugs,' recalls Susan, a recovering addict in her twenties. 'I started on softer drugs and at the time I said I'd never snort. I found myself before very long doing just that. Next I said I'd never take hard drugs, then I was taking cocaine. I always said I'd never touch heroin but it wasn't very long before I was taking heroin. Then I said I'd never inject. Then I started doing that.'

Sometimes, it's true, there are times when it seems as if the illness is getting better. Perhaps the addict manages to give up drugs for a time. Or for a few weeks he seems to control how much he takes. Yet in the long run these are only temporary reprieves in an ever downward slope.

Getting honest

If this is an illness which tells you that you haven't got it, how are you going to see the truth? How are you going to break through the inner denial?

Most addicts and alcoholics show this inner denial. They feel that they're different. They're not really addicts. They just take drugs. And they only take drugs because . . .

Because their parents didn't love them, because their parents smothered them with love, because they are unemployed, because their job is so stressful, because their families were rich, because their families were poor, because, because, because . . .

These aren't reasons. They are excuses. Every single one of them.

And to get well, addicts have to break through these excuses. They have to listen to that small voice within them which is still there. It may be only a tiny whispering voice. But it is telling them the truth – that they are ill and that they need help.

Honesty is what gets an addict well. The courage to be honest. The courage to look at what is really happening in his or her life.

Are you an addict or an alcoholic?

The simplest way to decide whether you are an addict or an alcoholic is to ask yourself what drugs or drink is doing to your life. You are an addict or an alcoholic if drugs or drink are causing problems in any of the following areas of your life – yet you are continuing to use drugs or drink:

1. Health.

2. Personal life.

3. Family life – either problems with your parents, with your partner, or with your children.

4. Social life.

5. Work or occupational life. People who do not do paid employment should ask themselves if drugs are affecting their housework, voluntary work or other activities.

6. Finance – look for debts, overcommitments, too much spent on drugs or drink.

7. Ethical behaviour.

These are the main categories in which drugs may be giving you problems. If you are an addict you may find it difficult to see the problems caused by drugs. So here are some more detailed questions, which cover the same kind of thing.

Are drugs causing problems in your life?

Try to answer these questions honestly. Those who are drinking should substitute the word 'alcohol' for 'drugs'.

1. *Do you need more drugs than you used to to get the same effect, or do you use drugs more often than you used to?*
In the first stages of their illness, addicts find that their use of a drug increases as their tolerance for that drug grows. They need more drugs to get high, or they need them more often. In the same way alcoholics may have a very hard head for alcohol,

priding themselves on out-drinking their companions. This is because their tolerance for alcohol is growing.

2. *Do you experience temporary memory lapses or difficulties in keeping track of time?*
Addicts find that they lose track of time, either because the drug is speeding them up, or because it is slowing them down so that they nod off. Alcoholics have memory lapses, when they cannot remember what they did or where they were. These are called 'blackouts'. As the illness gets worse, time difficulties and blackouts increase in number and their onset becomes more unpredictable.

3. *Have you ever sneaked extra supplies of the drug?*
Addicts often find they are sneaking off to their own room or to the lavatory in someone else's house to take more drugs while nobody notices. Or they may steal their friends' drugs. They may start searching other people's medicine cabinets, or smoking the cannabis plant being grown by someone else.

If they use alcohol, they will start trying to get extra drinks at a party or to sneak in an extra round.

4. *Are you preoccupied with drug-using?*
The mental obsession with drugs grows as the illness progresses. The addict begins to withdraw from those who do not use drugs, and to avoid their company. Most talk with fellow-users is about drugs, doing drugs, dealers and prices. Alcoholics talk about what they drank, pubs and drinking occasions. Other hobbies and interests fade away.

5. *Do you use drugs in a hurry?*
More and more the addict uses drugs for the effect, and wants that effect quickly. To that end, using becomes more urgent. In the haste, needles are not sterilised. Standards deteriorate. There is a compulsive need for instant gratification, and to get drugs as quickly as possible the addict will do all kinds of things he or she would not normally have done. Addicts or alcoholics have no idea of putting off pleasure. Just as a baby howls and screams when his rattle falls out of the pram, so an addict will lose emotional control if anything comes between him and his drugs.

6. *Are you reluctant to talk to non-users about your use of drugs?*
Addicts soon begin to avoid all references to their drug habit. They are reluctant to talk about it to non-users, and may be angry if the subject is raised. They feel that other people should mind their own business about their drug-use, and will make them feel

guilty about raising the subject. Alcoholics get angry if people suggest they drink too much.

7. *Do you sometimes lose control after the first drug or drink has been taken?*
Addicts begin to feel they need more as soon as they have taken the first drink or drug. Their control over how much they take begins to vanish. They may be compelled to finish whatever drug supplies are available – even when they know they will have run out of the drug in the morning. Alcoholics may have to finish the bottle, cannot leave the bar till it closes, are always the last at a party. This loss of control may not occur every single time – but the results of taking the first drug or drink become increasingly unpredictable.

8. *Do you find yourself inventing alibis, excuses, inventions or downright lies to explain your drug-using?*
Addicts soon begin to find alibis for their drug habit. They will rationalise their behaviour with a variety of excuses, reasons and explanations. These are invented to persuade themselves and others that they do not have a drug problem. Alcoholics behave in the same way.

9. *Have your family, or people you like, begun to say anything about your drug-using?*
As the illness progresses, family and friends begin to notice. Their concern may take the form of anxious suggestions of medical treatment, nagging, rows, coaxing, extorting promises, threats or entreaties.

10. *Have you begun to spend too much money, run up debts, started handing out advice to others or spending time on fantasies and schemes which never get accomplished?*
A sort of grandiosity sometimes begins to creep into the addict's lifestyle. Feelings of being superior to colleagues or family begin to grow. Addicts and alcoholics may spend money recklessly, buying extravagant cars or presents for others, entertaining beyond their means, or leading a lifestyle which is out of their financial reach.

11. *Do you experience feelings of growing anger, or increasing fits of frustration?*
A kind of inner anger or resentment begins to grow in the addict. Impatience and intolerance of others increases. The addict or alcoholic is increasingly touchy, over-sensitive or unable to take the slightest criticism.

12. *Do you have moments of remorse and guilt about your drug-using or your behaviour while using drugs?*
In the beginning feelings of remorse and guilt grow in addicts and alcoholics. These vary from the remorse which follows bad behaviour, to feelings of guilt and unease which may occur at any time, even if there seems to be no apparent reason. Under the influence of this remorse, resolutions to give up or promises of better behaviour are made – only to be broken. In the end, some addicts feel nothing and show no moral sense at all. In their drug-using they are looking for relief from pain rather than for pleasure.

13. *Do you have spells when you abstain from drugs?*
Addicts may change the pattern of their drug-using from daily using to spells of abstinence followed by using again. These days or weeks of abstinence may be part of a resolution to stop using – but there is always an excuse to start again. This can be a way of deluding themselves that they are not dependent. For there is a myth that if you can stop using drugs you are not an addict. But it is a myth, since all addicts can stop for a time. It is the way they start again, and again, and again that shows they are dependent. Alcoholics go on the wagon for a time in much the same way. Sometimes periods of abstinence – at home, in health farms or even in clinics and hospitals – are a way of trying to control the drug. After drying out and getting better physically, the addict feels able to start using again.

14. *Have you changed your pattern of using drugs?*
In the battle to control their using, many addicts start changing their pattern of using. They may switch from one drug to another, claiming it was the previous drug that caused problems. They may change from snorting to injecting in order to maintain or increase the high. Or they may start taking prescription drugs, including methadone, claiming that these cannot harm them. Alcoholics may start switching drinks, claiming that drinking beer or wine only is the way to control their drinking.

15. *Have you lost friends you had before using drugs?*
Childhood friends, or work friends made before using drugs, begin to drop away as the addict's life centres more and more around drugs. Friends are now chosen because of their mutual interest in drugs or drink.

16. *Have drugs affected your work?*
Trouble at work begins to show in the addict's life. Days lost through drug-use or drinking, warnings about irresponsible behaviour, or loss of promotion are the first signs. Later, jobs are

lost, or sometimes the addict or the alcoholic resigns from a job before being fired. Those who are self-employed start losing work or clients. As the illness progresses, addicts have to use drugs to function. Then they cannot function properly because they have used drugs. This is the illness – first addicts start using drugs and then drugs start using them. Or, as the old proverb has it – man takes a drink: drink takes the man.

17. *Has the attitude of your family and friends towards you worsened?*
Family and friends who were once anxious and concerned about the addict's drug-using or the alcoholic's drinking now begin to lose patience. Addicts and alcoholics may find they are now thrown out of the family home.

18. *Have you had medical treatment, hospital treatment or residential treatment of any kind for your drug-use?*
Addicts and alcoholics begin a round of medical establishments for their problem. Sometimes they are treated for drug dependence or alcoholism. At other times, doctors or clinics may diagnose them as suffering from depression or some other mental illness. These are often mistaken diagnoses and are convenient because they allow addicts to continue to deny their addiction.

19. *Do you feel growing resentments?*
The inner anger of the addict and alcoholic grows. He or she blames others for everything. Even small setbacks produce inappropriate fury and resentment.

20. *Have you tried changing jobs, changing friends, changing homes or changing countries to escape your problem?*
In an attempt to escape the growing pain of the problem, addicts and alcoholics start changing their outward circumstances. They may change jobs to avoid the stress that they themselves have created. They may change partners. They may try living in a new area in order to get away from dealers, drug-using friends, or drinking pals. They often start a new life abroad, in the hope that this will do the trick. Recovering addicts call this escape behaviour 'doing a geographical'. They do not realise that through all these changes they take themselves and their drug or drink problem with them.

21. *Do you protect your supply of drugs?*
Here are some of the things that addicts do to protect their supply: they have more than one hiding place for drugs or for bottles; they hide drugs even when they are living alone; they try to save part of the drug or drink for the next morning; they con the doctor into

giving them more than one prescription; they have more than one doctor in order to get more than one prescription; they keep a spare prescription in case they run out; they collect drug paraphernalia; they purchase more drugs or drink before their supplies run low.

22. *Do you use drugs to get you started in the morning?*
Some alcoholics start drinking in the morning just to get themselves together. In the same way, eventually addicts have to use drugs shortly after waking in the morning just to face the day.

23. *Do you do things under the influence of drugs that you would not have done before you started using drugs?*
The addict's behaviour begins to show signs of ethical deterioration. Drug-using affects behaviour. The addict may come to accept lower standards of behaviour. Often this behaviour is the direct result of being high; sometimes it will occur when the addict is in a period of temporary abstinence. Here are some of the things addicts and alcoholics have done while they were using or drinking: lied to loved ones; fiddled expenses; fiddled the housekeeping money; run up debts knowing they could not pay; stolen money from family; shoplifted; mugged people; had sex with people they did not like; had sex for money; stolen a friend's drugs. By the end, most addicts and alcoholics show total and utter disregard for themselves and others.

24. *Are you using drugs more or less continuously now?*
At the late stages of the illness, the addict may need to take drugs more or less continuously. Drugs are needed last thing at night, during the night, and first thing in the morning before getting out of bed. Addicts start keeping their supply by the bed. Alcoholics have a bottle within reach of the bed.

25. *Do you have indefinable fears?*
Addicts and alcoholics suffer from fear which has no reason to it. They may also have inexplicable anxiety and panic attacks. An appalling sense of impending doom afflicts them.

How to use this questionnaire

This is not a formal questionnaire and there are therefore no scores. However, its questions describe the progressive illness of chemical dependence.

Did *any* of the questions relate to you? Because if any of them did, you are dependent on drugs or alcohol. The more questions that apply to you, the worse the progression of your addiction or alcoholism.

Remember – an addict is somebody who goes on using drugs even though they are causing problems. An alcoholic continues to drink despite the problems drinking causes.

The questionnaire can also be used by the family and friends who suspect someone they love may have a problem with drugs or alcohol.

If you decide you have become dependent on a drug or on drink, do not be disheartened. Facing the reality of chemical dependence is the first step towards getting well.

Now read on to discover how you can recover from this illness.

5

Deciding to Come Off Drugs

If you think you may have a problem with drugs, act now. Even if you feel you have only the beginnings of a problem, act now.

For chemical dependence is an illness that can be terminal. Worse still, it is an illness which exacts more and more suffering from the addict or alcoholic as it progresses. With agonising inevitability it will drain from you your health, your happiness and every bit of self-respect.

Remember, chemical dependence is a progressive illness. Along its downward slide there may be moments of remission, but inevitably you will become more and more ill as the disease gets its grip on you.

Yet it is an illness that can be halted at any point. Indeed the rule is: *the earlier you stop taking drugs or drinking, the easier your recovery.*

The dangers of delay

Sadly, many addicts feel that there is no urgency about stopping their habit. They find excuses to put off action. Or they tell themselves that the problems are not that bad.

These delaying tactics mean that they become more ill, and their recovery becomes more difficult. Addicts or alcoholics who delay getting help are gambling with their lives, because this is an illness which can kill.

Look at it this way. If a woman finds a tiny lump in her breast, she immediately seeks help from her doctor in case it is breast cancer. The smaller the lump, and the earlier in her illness it is discovered, the more likely she is to recover from breast cancer.

But suppose she delayed, telling herself it couldn't be that bad yet. The lump would grow and the illness would spread. Every week that went by would diminish her chances of recovery. If she waited until the breast lump was a large suppurating sore, it could cost her her life.

This can happen to those who delay getting help for their drug or drink problem.

Here are some of the excuses addicts give, when they think they are not that bad.

1. They have not lost their job.
2. They have not lost the love of their families.
3. They have not lost their friends.
4. They have not lost their health.

'Yet' – the three-letter warning word

Have another look at those excuses for remaining ill. Are they that good? One way to put them in their proper perspective is to use the little three-letter word 'yet' at the end of them. Now they look very different.

1. You have not lost your job – yet.
2. You have not lost the love of your family – yet.
3. You have not lost your friends – yet.
4. You have not lost your health – yet.

With that little extra word, those excuses for doing nothing about the problem look very different. Those excuses look like urgent warnings.

So every time you find yourself using this kind of excuse, add the little word 'yet' to it. That single word might help save your life.

Hitting rock bottom

When you feel you just can't go on any longer, you have hit rock bottom. And it feels like the worst place in the world to be.

Everybody has a slightly different experience of hitting rock bottom. But most recovering addicts and alcoholics agree that until they have this feeling they are not forced to change. When at last they feel they can't go on any more as they are, then finally they are willing to get help.

Tracey's rock bottom came after trips to doctors, psychiatrists, casualty departments and even acupuncturists. She had finally been put in yet another treatment centre by her parents, but had been thrown out because of her disruptive and uncooperative behaviour.

'When my parents discovered what had happened, they told me to get lost,' she recalls. 'I was literally out on the streets. I didn't have a penny. I remember thinking "I've got two options. Either I've got to do something, or I'd better take a load of barbiturates and finish it now." A girlfriend took me to Narcotics Anonymous, and I started going to their meetings.' Her five years of drug-using ended that day. She now has a happy life.

Hitting rock bottom doesn't have to involve anything very dramatic. Elaine, a woman in her sixties, was dependent on tranquillisers which she topped up with a tumblerful of whisky every night. An almost trivial incident made her realise she had a drink and drugs problem.

'I had a horror of water in my flat, and a leak from the flat upstairs (as I thought) upset me. I called the plumbers and they found that the rug on the bathroom floor was completely wet. They told me that the bath must have overflowed and I wouldn't believe them. After they'd gone, I began to realise they must be right. I had been too knocked out by pills and booze to notice it at the time. I said to myself: "There must be something wrong. I can't go on like this." A few days later I went to my first Alcoholics Anonymous meeting.'

That incident was the straw that broke the camel's back. She suddenly realised that she was ill and that she needed help.

Missing the chance

Of course, you can let the chance slip by. Alison, a cannabis addict and alcoholic, remembers how she missed the chance to get well. 'At the age of twenty-five I was living with a rock group and we had a very hefty evening – a lot of drinks and a lot of drugs. A lot of dope. At 6.30 a.m. I got up dehydrated and did all the washing up, and I finished up some red wine, and then white wine and then cognac.

'By 11.30 a.m. I was in a suicidal depression, so I rang the office up and said "I'm going to kill myself." They sent round Susan, my friend. She arrived and I said to her, "I think I'm an alcoholic."

' "No, you're not," she said. "You're a nice girl."

'That was the moment when I could see I was suicidal because of the drinks and the drugs. I could make the connection, but because Susan said what she did, the moment passed. I went on drinking and taking dope for a further three and a half years.'

Many addicts and alcoholics have similar moments of truth, which they let slip by. How many times have you told yourself, 'I'll really do something about it'? And then you've done some more drugs or had a few drinks, and the feeling of urgency has evaporated.

It's the old excuse: 'I'll quit tomorrow.' But will you? Will you even get the second chance? Have you ever met an *old* addict? You haven't? Well, ask yourself why it is there aren't any old addicts.

Or perhaps you have decided you *will* act. You've told yourself you will stop using drugs or drinking. And you have – for a few days, perhaps even for a few weeks. But then you've hit a bad patch and you've gone back to drugs or drink. Or perhaps you simply decided you deserved a reward for good behaviour and started again with that excuse. And you've probably told yourself: 'It'll be different this time.'

If this is the case, we come to what is probably the single most important fact about giving up drugs.

YOU CAN'T DO IT ON YOUR OWN.

It is a statistical fact that very few addicts or alcoholics manage to give up drugs or alcohol without some kind of support system. Drugs or drink have been so important in their lives that when they stop using them there is a great gap in their way of life. Something has to take its place.

'I stopped lots of times,' recalls William, a recovering addict who has been clean and happy for three years. 'Each time stopping became harder, and the gaps between not using and using became shorter. I found that as the withdrawals got worse, I got more practised at handling them.

'But it was after the withdrawals – that was the worst. There was a sort of black hole in my life, a feeling of "What the hell's the point?" I'd get two or three weeks clean of withdrawals and be such a mess as a person that I'd go back to using.'

Addicts or alcoholics who try just to carry on, without putting anything in the place of drugs or alcohol, eventually fail. Sooner or later almost all of them go back to drugs or drinking.

After all, if chemical dependence is an illness, it needs some kind of extra care. If you went into hospital for an appendix removal, it would be madness to discharge yourself directly you came to after the operation. You simply wouldn't be well enough to plunge straight back into normal life. And besides, it would be crazy to try and take out the stitches yourself.

It is just the same with drug dependence. You are going to need proper after-care.

So if you want to get well, you are going to need help.

Asking for help

It's not enough to know you need help. You, yourself, have got to ask for it.

And the sooner you make that vital move, the better. For chemical dependence is a subtle and cunning disease. It will try to lure you into false optimism, and give you all kinds of reasons for not doing what will get you well.

If you are an addict whose partner or family has not yet given up hope, you may well already have had offers of help. They may have told you about clinics which can help you, or offered to go with you for expert help.

Or maybe among your friends is an addict who has successfully given up drugs and is living a new life. Or maybe you know an alcoholic who is leading a life without booze. Perhaps they told you about it and offered their help.

Take the help offered.

Maybe at the time it was offered, you indignantly refused. Maybe you feel embarrassed, or even angry, at the thought of having to change your mind and tell them you need help after all.

Don't let shame or guilt or false pride stop your chances of recovery. If you know where help is available, grab it with both hands.

The best kind of care is from other recovering addicts or alcoholics. They know what it is to stop using drugs or drink, and they have learned how to live life without them. You will find these in Narcotics Anonymous and in Alcoholics Anonymous.

Narcotics Anonymous and Alcoholics Anonymous

Narcotics Anonymous, which is made up of thousands of recovering addicts from all over the world, started in July 1953 when a bunch of addicts got together to help each other come off drugs and *stay* clean, in order to lead happy lives again.

In fact, it grew out of the experience of Alcoholics Anonymous, the self-help organisation for alcoholics which has been flourishing since 1935. AA discovered a secret which has revolutionised the treatment of alcoholism – the best person to help a drinking alcoholic is an alcoholic who has discovered how to stay sober.

In the same way, the best person to help an addict in the grip of chemical dependence is another addict who has discovered how to stay off drugs.

Narcotics Anonymous has no clinics or hospitals. It has no counsellors, no social workers, no policemen, no clergymen, no doctors or authority figures telling you what to do.

Narcotics Anonymous is just a bunch of ex-junkies and ex-pillheads helping each other stay off drugs. (Of course, there are social workers, policemen, clergymen and doctors in NA. But they are there because they too are addicts staying well.) It's just the same in Alcoholics Anonymous.

Will they report me to the authorities?

Addicts who are still using drugs usually come up against the law. Possession of drugs is illegal, and addicts often feel strong fears and resentments about policemen, magistrates and all authority.

'I regarded all policemen and magistrates as people to be avoided. Doctors were people to whom I'd describe ailments at length to see if I might just get some drugs out of them,' says Nick, who finally got help from a specialist clinic and then joined NA when he came out.

These fears are quite understandable. Many using addicts are breaking the law just by using the drugs they do. Others have to commit crimes to finance their using.

But these fears are *not* reasonable when it comes to getting well. If fear or hatred of authority stops you asking for the help you need, you are letting it hurt *you*.

Narcotics Anonymous didn't get their name by chance. The 'Anonymous' part of it means what it says. Every single member is anonymous. Nobody ever reveals who is a member.

NA isn't interested in your past. They don't care what you took, what your connections were, or how you financed your habit. They are only interested in helping you do something about your drug problem.

NA doesn't have anything to do with the authorities – with medical records, police records, or social-worker records. It doesn't have any bosses. And it doesn't charge any fees. It doesn't keep records of its members. Like Alcoholics Anonymous, it protects its members' anonymity completely.

You don't even have to have stopped using drugs or drink. All that you need to get NA's or AA's help is to *want to stop*.

How does it work?

Both Narcotics Anonymous and Alcoholics Anonymous hold meetings of recovering addicts and alcoholics – sometimes in church halls, sometimes in hospitals or clinics, occasionally in homes or social-service offices. Just wherever the rent is cheap!

If you decide you want their help, all you have to do is ring their number and they will put local members in touch with you, or tell you where the nearest meeting is.

Meetings vary in format, but a fairly typical NA meeting will usually have a secretary who runs the meeting, and a speaker. Often this speaker will say something about his addiction and how he recovered from it. Other NA members then join in, perhaps adding their comments or telling something about their own experience. Newcomers are not expected to speak at the meeting – though if they want to, they can. Alcoholics Anonymous meetings are run in the same way.

What if there is no NA where I live?

In all countries where it operates, NA has a central office which deals with enquiries. This office will tell you where there are local members.

If there is no NA, turn to Alcoholics Anonymous for help. AA has been going longer than NA and has a wider spread of offices. Often the local telephone book or the telephone operator will have their number. Local Samaritan offices usually have AA details too.

It may seem odd to send a drug addict to Alcoholics Anonymous, which is, strictly speaking, for people who have a problem with alcohol. But nowadays most AA meetings include members who have used both drink and drugs. They can help you.

Besides, AA membership is for everybody who wants to stop drinking alcohol. As the preamble to every AA meeting puts it: 'The only requirement for membership is a desire to stop drinking.'

Every addict should stop drinking alcohol, because *alcohol is a drug which alters the mood and is therefore addictive*. So any addict is entitled to attend AA meetings.

In that sense too, all addicts are entitled to call themselves alcoholics. And it is customary to preface all remarks at an AA meeting with 'I'm Michelle or Tom. I'm an alcoholic.'

Alison, the recovering addict and alcoholic we met earlier in this chapter, got well in Alcoholics Anonymous in 1977 before NA had started in Britain. 'At my first meeting I sat next to a man who talked about drugs and rock music. I think that helped me feel I was in the right place.'

That said, it has to be admitted that AA members sometimes feel uncomfortable with people who talk a great deal about drug-use. Graphic stories about fixing, scoring or pill-swallowing may even be met with the suggestion that AA is for those using alcohol, not other drugs.

It's partly a question of tact. If you want to use Alcoholics Anonymous to get well, it is best to play down stories of your drug-using at the meeting. Concentrate on talking about the methods of recovery.

'Some people go to AA and freak AA out with needle stories or with drug stories,' says Harry, the recovering addict whose story is told in Chapter 1. 'But that is the basis of their addiction anyway, as opposed to their dad's alcoholism. We say in NA, "Don't do that. Shut up about your drugs. Don't try to freak out the old boys in AA, because that's what you were doing outside. That's outside behaviour. So don't do it." '

And, if you feel you can't yet call yourself an alcoholic, just sit in the meeting and listen, rather than talk. This, anyway, is the best recipe for recovery in the early days. There's an AA saying: 'Take the cotton wool out of your ears and stick it in your mouth.' There will always be an opportunity to talk about drugs after the meeting in the informal get-togethers which most AAs have over tea or coffee.

Starting your own NA meeting

You can start your own Narcotics Anonymous meeting. All you need to do is to contact NA headquarters and they will help with advice.

It's probably best to start a new meeting with the help of another recovering addict. If you have been to local AA meetings and have met an AA member who used to use drugs as well as drink, ask if he or she will help. Many AA members have a history, if not of illegal drugs, then of being dependent on prescribed drugs like tranquillisers.

You should look out for a sympathetic member who is sober

and can give support. If possible, it should be somebody who has been sober for at least a year.

Recovering, not cured

It is extremely important to remember one vital fact: a drug addict or an alcoholic is *never* cured. Stopping drugs is only the first step towards recovery. You will need the maintenance help of continued NA or AA meetings to stay off drugs.

It is rather like having diabetes. Diabetes is an illness from which people can recover quite simply – by taking insulin. But if they stop taking their insulin, they relapse back into the active phase of the illness. Insulin helps them recover from diabetes, but it isn't a once-for-all cure. In the same way, Narcotics Anonymous will help you recover from your addiction, but it is not a once-for-all cure.

If you are attending NA or AA, you may find that is all you need to do. Many tens of thousands of women and men have recovered from chemical dependence in this way without needing any further help.

However, it is possible that you will need professional help at the time when you are stopping drugs. The next chapter deals with each drug in detail, and, as you will see, some drugs – *not* usually heroin, but drugs like tranquillisers, barbiturates and alcohol – should be stopped with medical help.

Getting a doctor to help

It's not always easy for an addict to find a doctor who will be helpful. Many doctors refuse to treat addicts who are using illegal drugs like heroin, cocaine and speed.

Luckily, many of these drugs don't necessarily need medical help for withdrawals. As you will see in the next chapter, coming off heroin, methadone and many of the illegal drugs is surprisingly safe.

Barbiturates are quite another thing. These drugs can give dangerous withdrawal symptoms, and therefore coming off them should *always* be done with medical help.

Those who are taking tranquillisers and alcohol should have medical help on coming off – if it's the right kind of help. The trouble is that the average family doctor doesn't necessarily know very much about chemical dependence.

Besides, if you already have a doctor, he may be the one who is giving you the tranquillisers on which you are dependent. Good doctors are usually happy when their patients ask for help in coming off their prescribed pills, but occasionally an out-of-date doctor is reluctant to help. Some do not want to admit that the pills are doing harm, or they do not know how to manage a withdrawal schedule for their patient.

If you think your doctor comes into this category, a chat with long-standing NA or AA members may help you find a new doctor who understands drug dependence better. Treating addicts and alcoholics is still something of a speciality in medicine, rather than general knowledge.

Some addicts need treatment in hospitals and clinics. They just can't seem to stop and stay stopped without this extra help.

Finding a clinic

Not all drug-dependence clinics are equally effective. Some are excellent, and many are reasonably helpful. They may give heroin addicts methadone, but it will only be for about a week – just for withdrawal.

Unfortunately, some clinics simply take addicts off their heroin and give them methadone instead for weeks or months at a time. *That's simply making a heroin addict into a methadone addict.* This kind of treatment will just delay your recovery. You will stay ill with the illness of chemical dependence. And, worse still, if you want to recover by giving up methadone, you will discover that its withdrawal effects are more prolonged than those of heroin.

Local NA and AA members often know the local clinics. They have a network of ex-patients who can report on the good – and the bad – clinics. Neither organisation officially recommends hospitals or clinics, but individual members are often good sources of advice about where the best local clinic is to be found.

You will find good and bad clinics within the health system, and you will find good and bad clinics in the fee-paying system. Just because a clinic charges high fees does not mean that it offers good treatment. In the same way, there is no automatic superiority among the health-service clinics.

What matters is the kind of treatment a clinic offers.

Checklist for finding a clinic

If you know of a clinic but are not sure what kind of treatment it offers, here are the questions you can ask them.

1. Is its treatment based on abstinence from all mood-altering drugs, including alcohol and prescribed drugs like methadone and tranquillisers?

2. Does it support the self-help groups Alcoholics Anonymous and Narcotics Anonymous? Some clinics have not yet heard of NA, but if they support AA this is a sign that they understand the principles of recovering from chemical dependence.

Just occasionally, you may be unable to find the right kind of clinic, yet you may feel you need supervised detoxification in a hospital setting. If so, you may have to use either an ordinary hospital to detox (rather than a specialised drug-dependence or alcoholism unit), or you may have to use a drug-dependence clinic which doesn't give the ideal treatment. You can always ask NA or AA members to visit you while you are there.

For the record, it is as well to know that detoxification should not last more than five to seven days. Any kind of treatment which involves more than about a week of taking other drugs as substitutes is delaying your recovery and is physically unnecessary.

The only exception to this is the treatment given to those who are on tranquillisers and barbiturates. With these prescribed drugs, withdrawal has to take place over a number of weeks, not days.

Remember – don't give up the drugs you use only to fall prey to others. It makes no sense at all. In particular, both methadone and tranquillisers, the drugs which are sometimes mistakenly prescribed for months at a time, are going to be harder to come off.

Coming off drugs – final checklist

1. Make the decision that you will ask for help to get off drugs.

2. Ring Narcotics Anonymous or Alcoholics Anonymous and co-operate with them in their efforts to get you help. Do this as a matter of urgency.

3. Get the help of doctors or clinics only if you need them and if they are recommended by seriously recovering people.

6

How to Stop: a Drug-by-Drug Guide to Withdrawal

Stopping using drugs is simple. Not easy, but simple. Anybody who really wants to stop using drugs or drinking can do so. Thousands of people are living examples of how it is done – and of the happiness that results from a life free from drugs and alcohol.

You can do it too. You've probably done it numerous times, but with all those past attempts to stay clean or stop drinking behind you, you are probably frightened of what may happen when you do try again.

Cold turkey is nonsense

The first thing is to put out of your mind all the bad movies, harrowing chapters in thrillers and newspaper stories which you have seen and read. Their descriptions of coming off drugs are usually so much rubbish.

The agonies of cold turkey are a myth. Coming off the so-called 'hard' drugs like heroin or methadone is not dangerous. Uncomfortable, perhaps – undoubtedly an uncomfortable experience. But not dangerous at all.

Oddly enough, it is the legal drugs that are likely to cause the worst withdrawal problems. Coming off alcohol is worse than coming off heroin, and can sometimes be dangerous. Coming off tranquillisers can be worse still. The only other risky drugs to come off are barbiturates and Heminevrin (chlormethiazole edisylate). Barbiturates are even more dangerous than tranquillisers.

So there is no need for people on illegal drugs like heroin, cocaine and so forth to fear withdrawing; it does help, though, if you understand a little about the process of coming off.

What are withdrawal symptoms?

These are the symptoms that occur when the drugs leave the body. Some drugs have a set pattern of withdrawal symptoms that occur in the body. Other drugs, like cocaine or amphetamines, which are said not to have any physical withdrawal symptoms, nevertheless have psychological symptoms that sometimes affect physical behaviour.

All addicts will have *some* withdrawal symptoms, whether physical or psychological. They are to be expected, and indeed they are a good sign: a sign that the drug is leaving the body – the first stage in recovering from chemical dependence.

Here is a drug-by-drug description of how to stop, what withdrawal symptoms to expect, and how best to deal with them.

Heroin, methadone, the other opiates and narcotic analgesics

How to stop

It is safe but uncomfortable just to stop taking heroin and the other opiates. There is absolutely no *dangerous* withdrawal reaction. If you are taking under half a gram of heroin or less than a quarter to half a gram of methadone, you will not really need any medication at all. Even over-the-counter medication should be avoided.

If you are taking more than this, you don't, strictly speaking, *need* medication. However, if you have a doctor who understands drug dependence, ask for Heminevrin (chlormethiazole edisylate) and Lomotil (diphenoxylate hydrochloride). Ask him to give you a prescription daily, rather than one for all the drugs at once. You should only take these drugs for three to seven days. They will ease the withdrawal symptoms.

It is dangerous to take heroin, methadone or any other opiate on top of these drugs.

Withdrawal symptoms

The myth that heroin or methadone addicts go through cold-turkey horrors is complete and utter drivel. Coming off heroin is relatively much less painful than coming off alcohol or tranquillisers. Some addicts deliberately exaggerate their withdrawal symptoms to obtain more detox medication.

You should expect to shiver and shake for three or four days, with symptoms rather like those of 'flu – sweating, aches and pains, stomach cramps and a temperature. Tears, a running nose and yawning are also common. You will probably also have diarrhoea.

These are unpleasant, but they are minor symptoms. And, of course, there will be cravings for the drug.

Advice

Keep somebody with you, if possible, for the first few days. They are not needed in case of withdrawal danger, but simply to help you stop running to the dealer! Having company also helps ease the strong feelings of loneliness and isolation.

Keep occupied. Go to at least one Narcotics Anonymous or Alcoholics Anonymous meeting every day, if there is one. If you are with recovering addicts, you will get understanding about cravings and help in staying away from dealers and drug-using friends.

If you are working, you will need two or three days off work. But get back to work as soon as possible. Staying alone doing nothing is dangerous because it makes it easier to give in to the cravings.

Do not substitute other drugs or drink. After you have finished the drugs prescribed for the three to seven days of withdrawal, you should not take any drugs or alcohol.

Cocaine

How to stop

Just stop. There is no dangerous withdrawal reaction to stopping cocaine.

Withdrawal symptoms

There will be the down feeling, the depression, that normally follows the high. Heavy users feel severely depressed. Some users also feel giddy when they stop. Many feel acutely paranoid. They also feel physically agitated, which is an unpleasant experience.

Advice

Get to as many meetings of Narcotics Anonymous or Alcoholics Anonymous as you can, preferably at least once a day. If there is somebody with you for the first two or three days of coming off, that will help you stay away from dealers and drug-using friends. Taking some exercise will help dissipate the physical tension and make sleeping easier.

Do not substitute other drugs or drink.

Amphetamines and other stimulants

How to stop

Just stop. There is no dangerous withdrawal reaction to stopping amphetamines.

Withdrawals

You are likely to feel exhausted and depressed – just as you normally do when you come down from the drug. An insatiable hunger, known as 'the munchies', often follows withdrawal. Some people have stomach cramps. If you have developed delusions, paranoid ideas or hallucinations, these may take several months fully to disappear and you will need specialist psychiatric treatment.

Advice

Get to as many meetings of Narcotics Anonymous or Alcoholics Anonymous as you can.

Do not substitute other drugs or drink.

Glue sniffing and other solvents

Just stop. There are no dangerous withdrawal reactions from glue sniffing or from most of the other solvents. Withdrawal symptoms such as sickness, depression, insomnia and loss of appetite sometimes occur. Get to Narcotics Anonymous and do not substitute other drugs or alcohol.

Cannabis

How to stop

Just stop. There are no dangerous withdrawal reactions from cannabis.

Withdrawal symptoms

Heavy users have reported irritability, insomnia, nausea, loss of appetite and restlessness. You will get the emotional confusion and cravings that come to all addicts.

Advice

Despite the idea that cannabis is a 'soft' drug, it can be highly addictive for people who are regular users. Your recovery will need just as much effort on your part as a heroin addict's recovery from heroin. Make sure you get to Narcotics Anonymous meetings, where you can find other cannabis addicts.

Be careful not to substitute drink or other drugs.

LSD and hallucinogens

How to stop

Just stop. There are no dangerous withdrawal reactions to stopping LSD.

Withdrawal symptoms

You will feel only the normal psychological withdrawal symptoms experienced by all addicts.

Advice

Get to as many meetings of Narcotics Anonymous and Alcoholics Anonymous as possible.

In the first few days after stopping LSD, addicts may not feel much desire for the drug. This is likely to come a little later, so be prepared to resist these feelings.

Do not drink or substitute other drugs.

PCP or phenocyclidine

Just stop. There are no withdrawal symptoms, other than the psychological symptoms common to all addicts. Get to Narcotics Anonymous meetings and be careful not to substitute other drugs or drink.

Tranquillisers and sleeping pills (not barbiturates)

How to stop

First check exactly what you are taking by reading the name of the drug from the bottle in which it has been prescribed. Nowadays most tranquillisers and sleeping pills are from the benzodiazepine family of drugs. You will find the brand names in Appendix 1.

But if you have been taking the same tablets for years and years, your doctor may still be prescribing barbiturates for you. You can find this from Appendix 1. If so, follow the advice given for barbiturates later in this chapter.

If you are taking benzodiazepine tranquillisers or sleeping pills, *do not stop abruptly*: it is dangerous. You will need to cut down the drug over four to six weeks – or longer if you are taking a very high dose.

Doctors are becoming more knowledgeable about tranquilliser dependence (which is not necessarily tranquilliser abuse), and the doctor who is prescribing you the pills will probably help you cut down your dose. But if you are unlucky enough to have an out-of-date doctor, he may simply suggest you switch from one kind of tranquilliser to another. This will simply prolong the illness of tranquilliser dependence.

In Appendix 1 is a list of all the named tranquillisers and sleeping pills, and their normal doses. From this you can calculate how to cut down your dose safely.

Withdrawal symptoms

These include insomnia, anxiety, panic attacks, muscle pain, depression, seeing or hearing things that are not there, dizziness, abnormal sensitivity to noise, touch and smell, a feeling of weakness, heart palpitations, dry mouth and a feeling of having an enlarged tongue. There is also the sensation that you have a tightening band round your head.

Some of the symptoms seem to be minor ones, but they are nevertheless rather strange. Some people have a metallic taste in the mouth, or experience the feeling that buildings are going to fall on them or that the ground under their feet is not solid. Muscles may twitch uncontrollably.

If this sounds a horrifying list of symptoms, take heart. Most people only suffer from three or four of them. The problem is that the withdrawal symptoms can confuse you into thinking the old anxiety (for which you were originally prescribed the pills) is back again.

It isn't. Though the symptoms can last for several weeks (even months if you have been on the tablets for years and years), all the anxiety and confusion of withdrawal will settle down eventually.

Advice

Get to Narcotics Anonymous or Alcoholics Anonymous meetings and find somebody who has been through the same experience. That way, you will get the understanding you need.

Be careful not to substitute drink or any other drug for tranquillisers.

Barbiturates

How to stop

If you are addicted to barbiturates, *stopping abruptly is extremely dangerous*. You must have medical supervision. Most doctors know about barbiturate dependence, and will help you stop.

If you are not sure what kind of pills you are taking, there is a list of barbiturate and other sedative drugs in Appendix 1.

Withdrawal symptoms

If the pills are withdrawn too rapidly, withdrawal symptoms from barbiturates can include delirium, hallucinations and fits. That is why withdrawing from barbiturates must be done under medical supervision. Other symptoms include restlessness, cramps, sickness and vomiting, shaking, insomnia and a feeling of great weakness.

Advice

Consult your doctor or find a clinic that can help you withdraw safely from these drugs.

Get to as many Narcotics Anonymous and Alcoholics Anonymous meetings as possible. After withdrawal, make sure you do not substitute benzodiazepine tranquillisers or sleeping pills for barbiturates. Stay off all drugs and alcohol. Occasionally, doctors take the view that this does not matter, but it is folly to risk getting addicted all over again. Coming off tranquillisers is extremely painful, and it will mean having to go through withdrawal twice.

Patent medicines and analgesics

Just stop using them, and get to as many Narcotics Anonymous or Alcoholics Anonymous meetings as you can. Withdrawal symptoms may include restlessness, anxiety and twitching.

Do not substitute other drugs or alcohol.

Alcohol

How to stop

If you are regularly drinking heavily and have been dependent on alcohol for a long time, stopping without any medication has risks. You must have medical supervision.

Withdrawal symptoms

Feeling or being sick, shaking, sweating and cramps are common. Agitation, restlessness and lack of concentration are also part of the withdrawal symptoms. Most people experience insomnia. The first three days are the worst.

DTs – or *delirium tremens* – is the name given to really violent withdrawal shakes, which are sometimes accompanied by seeing or hearing things that are not there. Alcohol withdrawal fits can follow. That is why alcoholics should have some medical help in withdrawal. If these fits are not prevented or dealt with properly, they can be fatal.

Advice

Get to Alcoholics Anonymous, and try to attend their meetings daily if possible. A week off work will probably help you in the first days of your recovery, but get back to normal functioning as soon as possible.

If you are on more than one drug . . .

Mixtures of drugs, or drugs and alcohol, are fairly common among addicts. This may mean you are not sure how to stop. The rule of thumb is simple. If you are habitually using alcohol, barbiturates, or benzodiazepine tranquillisers with any of the other drugs listed here, you must take measures to avoid withdrawal fits by withdrawing *only under medical supervision*.

Psychological withdrawal symptoms

All addicts will get psychological symptoms when they stop using drugs. These are painful but not dangerous.

1. *Cravings for the drug.* These may be constant throughout the day or they may hit you at odd moments. They may feel overwhelming, but they are not. Think of them as a kind of trick the drug is playing on you. It wants you back as a user! Rule number one about coming off drugs – do not act on the cravings.

2. *Emotional confusion.* Mood swings are common in the first few days of withdrawal. You may swing from elation to suicidal depression, or from happiness to fury. All kinds of unpleasant feelings emerge as the drug leaves your system. Fear and anxiety are common. These emotions are painful, but in themselves they cannot hurt you. Keep reminding yourself that they will not last for ever.

3. *Minor aches and pains.* These have normally been blotted out by your drug-using; now they hit you with a surprising force. Addicts are not used to this kind of physical pain, because they generally blot it out with drugs. But pains like this are a sign that you are at last in touch with your own body.

4. *Agitation, restlessness, and extreme fatigue.* The mind seems unable to concentrate, and the body unable to relax. Yet, paradoxically, you may feel absolutely exhausted. Thinking is unclear. You may be unable to settle to anything.

5. *Fear*. Many addicts have feelings of fear that almost overwhelm them. They are terrified that they will not be able to stay off the drug. They are frantic at the thought that they may not be able to resist it and, on the other hand, they fear a life without drugs. That is why it is a good idea to spend as much time as possible at Narcotics Anonymous or Alcoholics Anonymous meetings. Stay in the company of recovering addicts as much as you can – or with friends or family who will support you and understand what you are going through.

6. *Insomnia*. Several nights of sleeplessness are common when you first come off drugs. You may find that you cannot get to sleep at all, and that you stay awake throughout the night. This is extremely unpleasant, but fundamentally it does not harm you. Nobody dies from lack of sleep. Sometimes the recovering addict is hit by nightmares or complex, disturbing dreams. This is often the brain catching up on dreaming (which it needs to do to stay healthy) because drugs have suppressed dreams for some time.

How to cope with withdrawal symptoms

Withdrawal symptoms are extremely unpleasant. Indeed, this is often why people stay on drugs in the first place – to avoid withdrawal pain. Addicts are particularly bad at living through pain, because they have used their drugs to escape unpleasant reality.

Yet if you want to get well, you will have to learn to cope with the first few days of withdrawal. You have probably done it before. Thousands of recovering addicts have discovered the fundamental principles of coping with withdrawal. If they can do it, you can do it too.

1. *A craving for the drug does not mean you have to take the drug.* Live through the craving. It is possible to live through persistent, even continuous, craving for days or weeks. In the next chapter we will give you some mental tricks that will carry you through.

2. *Live through the feelings of discomfort.* Addicts who are using drugs are often very bad indeed at enduring pain, whether it is physical or emotional pain. They are used to blotting it out with drugs. So the trick of coming off drugs is to learn to live through the pain – literally to endure it. This is why it is important to keep busy going to NA or AA meetings in the first few weeks. It helps distract the mind from the pain. Comfort yourself with the thought of how this discomfort will last only a few days.

3. *Talk about what you are going through*. This is another reason for going to NA and AA meetings. The illness of chemical dependence can partially be talked out of the system in these meetings. Share your pain with others, and you will find that it has diminished in its intensity.

4. *Withdrawal symptoms are a sign of recovery*. This is the good news. The drug-using addict doesn't suffer from withdrawal – only the *recovering* addict has these discomforts. They are the first signs of the body, mind and heart coming out of the illness. Keep remembering this. Remember too that there is a lot of happiness awaiting you.

5. *You only have to do it once*. You will never have to go through this withdrawal pain again, if you put your heart and soul into recovery. Unlike all the bad times on drugs, this bad time when you are getting clean and sober is a once-and-for-all experience.

You can recover

No matter how painful it feels, you *will* recover. In the next chapter we will tell you how to get through the first few weeks.

7

The First Few Weeks Off Drugs or Drink

Now stop.

Just don't take any more of the drug. Say 'No' to yourself and to your using or drinking friends. It's as simple as that. Concentrate with every fibre of your being on not taking the next fix, pill, smoke or drink.

Do that **NOW**.

(Or, if you are on a programme of cutting down tranquillisers, make sure that the next pill is the right cut-down dose as part of the programme. Tranquilliser addicts and barbiturate addicts reading this chapter will need to bear in mind that the abrupt stop which all other addicts should be doing does not apply to them. Alcoholics, too, must remember that abruptly stopping, without any medication for withdrawal, can be dangerous.)

The first few hours and days are not going to be easy. However, you will get through them successfully if you practise the skills of Narcotics Anonymous and Alcoholics Anonymous. These are truly lifeline mental tricks, designed to keep you clean and sober despite the pain of withdrawal.

The 24-hour plan

Give up drugs and drink just for the day – the day you are in now or the twenty-four hours that started from your last drug.

Everybody – yes, literally every single addict and alcoholic – can give up drugs or drink for a day. You may have done it many times – times when you couldn't get your supply of drugs or drink, or times when you were making those promises to yourself: 'I'll never do that again.'

This mental trick concentrates all your energies where they should be – on staying away from drugs *now*. It also means that you can stop worrying about tomorrow, or next week, or how you will manage next Christmas.

Most addicts cannot envisage staying off drugs for life. Indeed, if they think of it in that way, they simply become downhearted, or even downright unwilling to try. But you do not have to think in terms of a lifetime.

This forward thinking is what NA calls 'projection', and it's a killer. Thinking forward to all the difficulties that lie in the future fills your head with fear and despair, making it too much for you. So don't do it.

All you have to do is get through today without a drug. Thinking about giving up drugs for just one day, the day you are in, is much less worrying. Just concentrate on that.

Push tomorrow out of your head. And push yesterday out of your head too. Thinking back to the past will fill your head full of either dangerously euphoric memories or guilt and anxiety. Yesterday is no concern of yours just now.

Today is the only day that matters. And today is the day that you are going to get through without a drug.

Sometimes, when the cravings get very bad, you will probably feel you can't even manage a day without drugs. This is the moment when you start living not just twenty-four hours at a time, but ten minutes at a time.

The 10-minutes-at-a-time plan

In the first few days, you will probably have moments when you feel that you are going to use drugs literally any moment now. The craving is so strong that you feel almost – but not quite – overwhelmed by it.

This is when to live ten minutes at a time. Tell yourself that you will get through the next ten minutes – or five minutes, if necessary – without taking the drug. *Postpone* taking the drug or picking up the drink just that long.

You can do that. Undoubtedly, you can get through ten minutes without using drugs.

And when that ten minutes is over, start the next ten minutes without taking the drug.

Use the strength of recovering addicts

Before stopping, you should have made contact with NA or AA. Now use the strength of the recovering addicts and alcoholics who have successfully stayed clean and sober.

They've done it themselves. They know what you're going through. And, better still, they know *how* they did it. So listen to what they say and pick up the tips you need.

Get to as many meetings of these two groups as you possibly can. If you can fit in two a day, well do so. If you can manage only one a day, well that's fine too.

If there are both NA and AA where you live, go to the NA meetings first; then, if there are not many NA meetings, top up with the AA meetings as well if you are an addict. Addicts and alcoholics may not share the same experience of drugs and drink, but their experience of recovering is more or less identical. Addicts can learn from recovering alcoholics, and alcoholics can learn from recovering addicts.

But the most important thing of all is to get to meetings. It doesn't matter if you don't quite follow what is going on. It doesn't matter whether you like them or loathe them. Just get your body there, stick your bottom on the seat, and listen.

These meetings are the single most important part of recovering from the illness of chemical dependence. Without them you have little chance of remaining clean and happy. With them you have the best chance possible.

If you live in an area where there aren't many meetings, you may have to travel miles. Do so. If you haven't got a car, use trains, buses and taxis. They're expensive, but so was your drug habit. Getting to meetings is truly worth a small fortune.

Besides, you would do anything to get drugs or drink. You went to any lengths to go on using drugs or to go on drinking. Now go to any lengths to get well. Remember Ricky, whose story was told in Chapter 1. Because he didn't have any money he walked five miles to get to his first AA meeting.

At first the meetings may seem strange to you. You will need to go five or six times to start getting to know the other addicts there. It's just like joining a club. You don't know anybody at first, but once you start going regularly, you make friends.

Use the phone

At your first meeting, the other people there will offer you their phone numbers. Take them. Take every single phone number you can get and use it.

You may feel: 'I shouldn't ring. They were just being kind. They won't want to be bothered.'

This is the kind of thinking that interferes with your recovery. People who gave you their phone numbers did so in expectation that you would ring them. You are helping them to remember when they needed help.

And it is the phone that will give you a lifeline at the times you are not at meetings. You can ring if a craving suddenly hits you at work. You can ring first thing in the morning before you go to work. Or you can ring last thing at night, when you are perhaps alone and frightened.

Pick up the phone instead of picking up drugs or drink.

This is an NA and AA saying that has kept many an addict and alcoholic clean and sober. But the idea is to pick up the phone before, not after.

Stay away from the drug

The first thing to do is to clear out your living quarters. Throw any pills, medicines, drink or drugs down the lavatory and flush them away. Chuck away your gear – syringes, pipes, rolls of foil, cigarette papers, the lot. (Start smoking ready-mades if you smoke.)

Here are some other things that NAs and AAs have done in order to make sure they were not tempted by the nearness of drugs or drink.

1. They have changed their phone numbers so that dealers, or drug-using and drinking friends couldn't ring.

2. They have torn the phone numbers of drug-using friends and drinking pals and dealers out of their address books and made a point of actively forgetting them.

3. They have taken a new route to work or to social security, to make sure they didn't pass old haunts associated with drug-taking, or to keep away from pubs they used to drink in or off-licences they used to buy from.

4. They have avoided drug users and drinkers. (We will come to the matter of real friends later.)

5. They have stayed away from the cafés, pubs and clubs where they used, met other drug users, met dealers, dealt themselves, drank or met drinking friends.

6. They have kept away from pop concerts, parties, dinner parties and all other occasions where using drugs or drinking might be expected. Even the atmosphere of drug-using is dangerous for addicts who have just come off. Drinking situations are dangerous for alcoholics just off the booze.

Stick with the winners

Hang around with recovering addicts and alcoholics as much as possible – preferably with people who have been clean and sober for longer than you. These are the ones who can tell you how they did it.

The longer people have been clean or sober, the better they are for you. These are the winners.

Some people at NA and AA are still sick. They are not yet winners. Some still haven't managed to stop using drugs or drink. Others are off it so recently that they are still confused. These people need help themselves.

Then there are your friends. Well, which friends? The ones you used drugs with or drank with? It's a fair bet that some of them, at least, are just fellow-users or drinking pals.

'Of course they're my friends,' you think. But, friends or not, they are no good for you at the moment. Anybody using drugs or drinking must be avoided like the plague in the first few weeks of recovery.

For an addict who has just stopped using drugs, it is risky to have *any* contact with people who are still using them. Just knowing that somebody has drugs on them could be enough to tempt you back into using.

Going into pubs or being around heavy drinkers is not good for recovering alcoholics in the first few weeks. For a start, there's the smell of booze. Then there's the temptation when people offer you drinks.

If you live with a drug user or a drinker, you should consider moving out, at least temporarily. If you are married to one or related to one, it may be that you should nevertheless have some time away from their company. Putting yourself in a clinic is one answer. Very few people indeed manage to stay off drugs or drink when their partner is still on them or is drinking heavily. Nearly all need to get away for at least a few days or weeks before they can start recovering.

Outside friends and family can be a great help to you in the first few days if they know what is happening and understand about addiction and alcoholism. They will love you and support you, and generally help you through the first few bad days.

But some outside friends don't understand. It's not that they are drug users or alcoholics themselves; it is just that they don't realise the real facts of addiction.

They may try to 'cheer' you up by telling you that you are not really an addict. Or they may generally sabotage – without meaning to – your efforts at getting well. Avoid them. Later on, when you are better, you can get back in touch, but you don't need them in the first difficult days and weeks.

Putting your drug problem first

The other secret of successfully staying clean is to make your drug or drink problem your first priority. Make sure that you concentrate all your efforts and energies upon it. For the time being, let other problems lapse.

'I can't possibly do that,' you may think. 'My partner is threatening to leave. I'm overdrawn at the bank. There's my court case coming up next month. These are all far worse problems. I've got to do something about all of them urgently. They are much more important than my drug-using or drinking.'

This kind of thinking will keep you ill. It really will. Getting off drugs, and staying off them, is so full of possible set-backs that it simply has to be given absolute priority.

Think it out. If you go back to drugs and drink, what will happen? Your partner will almost certainly leave you eventually anyway. Your finances will undoubtedly get worse. You will make a worse impression at court, and you will probably get into more trouble with the law.

There isn't a single problem that a drug or a drink will make better. They will only make your problems worse.

If, on the other hand, you manage to stay off drugs and drink, you stand a far better chance of solving the problems in the long run. You can demonstrate to your partner that you are clean and sober. You can go to the bank manager and tell him how you are recovering from the illness of addiction, and work out a plan to put your finances on a proper footing. You can show the court that you are finally doing something about the drug-using or drinking that got you into trouble.

All these ways of dealing with the problems depend on your staying clean. So it makes perfect sense to put your drug or drink problem first.

Besides, in the first few days of coming off drugs or booze you are simply not well enough to solve the other problems of living. You may *feel* capable, but the truth is that your thinking and your emotions are confused.

So for the time being, just concentrate on staying off drugs and drink. Put the other problems aside for these first few days.

Remember the bad times

One of the ways to help you get through the first few days is to do something about that mind of yours. You may truly want to stop using drugs or drinking, and yet your mind seems to be full of 'funny' thoughts about using again or about taking a drink.

Remember, addiction is a psychological illness. Your mind got addicted to drugs and alcohol too. It may be trying to sabotage your efforts in order to get back to the drugs or the drink that it craves.

'It was as if my mind was divided into two. Part of it, the real me, wanted to stop and get better. But the other part wanted to go on drinking. I would have thoughts that perhaps I wasn't really an alcoholic. Or thoughts about drinking again would come into my mind. It's not easy to explain. But I had to make sure somehow that I was on the side of the sane part of my mind – the part that wanted to get well. I had to try and replace the drinking and using thoughts with thoughts that helped me stay sober,' is how one recovering alcoholic puts it.

One way to think yourself well is to remember all the bad things about using and drinking. When the thoughts about the good times come into your mind, replace them with the thoughts about the bad times.

'Don't let anybody tell you that using drugs isn't fun in the beginning: it is,' says one addict. 'But don't let anybody tell you it's fun to steal from your mother's purse, to see your sister crying, to become a homosexual prostitute to get money for drugs.'

The bad things that happened to you can help you get well – if you keep them in your mind during these first few days. One housewife who was addicted to tranquillisers wrote out a list of these things and put it on her fridge door to remind herself why she was giving up the pills.

Use the bad memories. If there's something particularly degrading that drugs or drink led you to, cherish that awful memory. Every time you get a tempting thought about going back to drug-taking or drinking, replace it with that bad memory. It will remind you why you should not take drugs or drink.

Thinking it through

The other mental trick is to think through what will happen if you take a drink or drug. Usually when a craving hits you, you think of the first part of drug-using – the pleasurable fix, the first joint or the first drink.

But using drugs or drinking doesn't end there. You don't stop at one fix, or one joint, or just one small glass of sherry! After the first enjoyable bit comes the excess, the drugged behaviour, the drunkenness, the passing out, the coming to, the withdrawals, and the appalling hangovers.

And with all these things comes the rest of drug-using and drinking – upsetting the ones who love you, lying, cheating, conning, stealing money, and all the other things addicts and alcoholics have to do in order to support their habit. All these things follow from the first use or the first drink.

When a craving hits you, and you think about the first joys of using, think it through – past the initial pleasure right to the pain that follows.

Hungry, angry, lonely, tired – H.A.L.T.

The craving for drugs or drink is likely to hit you at your weakest moments. That is why NA and AA have evolved this simple acronym: H.A.L.T.

If you are hungry, angry, lonely or tired, you are likely to want drugs. So you must avoid being these things by eating properly, by keeping with supportive people, and by getting the rest you need.

Anger is a particularly dangerous emotion for recovering addicts, because it turns so easily into self-destruction, and self-destruction is the habitual way of life for a drug-using addict or a drinking alcoholic.

Therefore you will have to try to avoid anger, if possible. If you think people or situations are likely to make you feel angry in these first few days, stay away from them. Walk out of the room rather than stay to have a row with somebody.

Of course, sometimes you are going to get angry. When that happens, deal with it immediately. Phone a fellow NA or AA about it. Or tell it all to a trusted friend, one who will be sympathetic but won't let you go too far in blaming others. The aim is to get rid of the anger, not to increase it.

Talk it out. Dump it at a meeting. You'll be surprised how much you calm down once you've got it out in the open.

If the anger is still there after talking about it to fellow-members, try physical exercise. Go for a swim, for a jog, or for a brisk walk. Chop wood or furiously dig the garden. Sweat out the anger through bodily exercise. You'll find it helps. Then talk about it some more to recovering addicts till it goes completely.

The danger in anger is that it will fester inside you, growing stronger and stronger. There's an NA saying: 'A resentment buried is a resentment buried alive.' Don't let the sun go down on your anger. Sitting and simmering is the worst thing you can possibly do.

Be kind to yourself

In these first few days you are going to feel pretty confused and ill. You can give yourself the tender care you would give to somebody you loved.

Eat nice food – whatever tempts you. Keep eating sweets. Put a bar of chocolate in your pocket or handbag and munch it when the cravings trouble you. Don't try to diet in the first few weeks of coming off. A few extra pounds of weight is a million times better than going back to using or drinking.

Hot sweet tea with two spoonfuls of sugar is the best thing if you have a hangover as part of stopping using drink or drugs. You may not like the sugar, but drink it. You need it.

Drink plenty of liquid, just as long as it doesn't contain alcohol. If you have been using alcohol as well as drugs, make sure there is a large quantity of soft drink in the house. Most people find they crave sweet things during withdrawal.

Have fruit juice or cola in the fridge ready to drink, with ice in hot weather. Fruit juice mixed with soda makes a good sparkling drink. Try a hot drink of blackcurrant juice with boiling water last thing at night, or a traditional cosy nightcap such as malted milk.

If you are a cigarette smoker, this is not the moment to cut back on fags. Although smoking isn't good for you, it may help you get through withdrawals. So don't do anything foolish like giving it up when you are coming off drugs.

Finally, pamper your body with long hot baths, aftershave, cologne and scent. If you are female, have your hair done. Small morale-boosters are a help in these early days. If you are clean outside, it will help you feel clean inside.

Fear and panic

Amazing fears often hit addicts in their first few days of not using. Sometimes they are utterly terrified that they are going to use drugs again.

And they are just as terrified of not using. Occasionally the fears are just indefinable. They seem to come and go from nowhere.

The fear of using drugs or drinking again is not all bad. Rightly handled, it can help you stay off them. Addicts and alcoholics ought to fear the power and lure of drugs and drink. A healthy fear will help them stay away.

But sometimes this fear is so intense that it seems almost to attack the inner defences against using. If you feel this kind of fear, this is the moment to use the phone and ring an NA or an AA. If you are without their phone numbers, ring the office number at the back of this book.

'I remember feeling absolutely terrible in the early hours of the morning,' recalled one recovering addict. 'I didn't know what to do. I could have rung an NA friend, but I was frightened to do so. I didn't realise that they wouldn't have minded. Instead I rang the NA number. Just hearing the recorded announcement did something to soothe my fears.'

Picking up NA and AA literature and reading it can also help in moments of panic. Keep a pamphlet in your pocket or in your handbag for these moments. The AA serenity prayer can help too – even if you don't believe in God. Many new members have found considerable comfort in that prayer, even if they are convinced atheists.

For the simple repetition of familiar words can help in moments of fear. It is as if they deflect the mind from its panic. A prayer, a poem, a slogan – almost anything will do. Repeat it over and over again, either out loud or in your mind like a mantra. The repetition will act as a way of calming you. Then get to a meeting just as soon as possible.

Hang on in there – no matter what

If you are using the 24-hour plan, and the 10-minutes-at-a-time plan for bad moments, you will get through somehow.

Sometimes the first few days are full of dreadful moments. You find you cannot work at anything. Your head is all over the place. You cannot sleep. You cannot relax. And yet you are horribly, appallingly exhausted all the time.

Naturally this means that you may not cope too well. You may find that very small set-backs such as missing a bus make you want to cry or rage. There may be difficulties at home or at work. None of these matter in the long run – as long as you do not use drugs or pick up a drink.

Whatever happens, whatever crises occur, whatever you do or don't do, in the long run you are doing all right if you're staying clean. Every day is a triumph for an addict who manages to stay away from drugs and for an alcoholic who stays sober.

So don't put yourself down. Remember that even if the world seems to be falling apart around you, everything will come out right in the end – just as long as you manage to stay away from drugs or drink.

If you are staying clean and sober, you are in there with a good chance, no matter how terrible you feel. If you go back on the bottle or back to using drugs, then that chance has utterly vanished.

Elation and over-confidence

Sometimes addicts and alcoholics feel surges of wild elation in the first few days of staying off drugs. They may decide that they've beaten the problem, that they don't need any more help, and that they can do without NA or AA.

This absurd over-confidence may lead them to take even more risks. They may hang around drug users, dealers or pubs. Their over-confidence may fool them into thinking that they can handle these situations. Sooner or later – and it's usually sooner – they go back to drugs or drinking.

If you feel wild elation and confidence, remember that this may be another trick of the mind in its attempts to get back to the drug it loves. Suspect your own feelings. Be extra cautious about your recovery.

Make sure that you do your recovery the safe way – going to lots of NA and AA meetings, staying away from drugs and drug users, drink and drinkers, and trying to do the things that recovering people suggest.

Don't take risks with your new-found recovery. Chemical dependence is an extremely subtle illness. The greatest danger it poses is that of relapse.

Difficulty in stopping

Some people have great difficulty in stopping in the early days of going to NA or AA. They should not despair. If they talk frankly about it to the recovering addicts, they will probably find somebody else who had the same problem – and yet who is now clean and well.

The most important thing is not to lie about your using or drinking. If you lie to other recovering addicts and alcoholics, you cut yourself off from the help you need. If you can be honest about the fact that you are still using or drinking, then you will find great kindness and help from NA and AA members. Some of them had the same difficulty in stopping.

People who find they cannot seem to stop, despite going to NA and AA meetings, should consider whether going into a specialist clinic or hospital might help them. Sometimes a few weeks away helps stop the habit of using or breaks the continued drinking. Ask recovering people which clinics or hospitals helped them.

If this is your problem, turn back to page 77 for advice on finding a good clinic. If you cannot find a clinic, then see if yet more meetings might help you.

But many people who have difficulty in stopping are not really doing what is suggested. They are not going to enough meetings, or they are not using the phone to make contact between meetings. They are simply not putting into practice what recovering addicts suggest.

Remember, if you are not actually using drugs or drinking this very minute, then you have stopped. *All you have to do is not to start again*.

Your twenty-four hours can start from *now*. All you have to do is to concentrate your efforts on not taking the next pill, drink, fix or smoke – just for today.

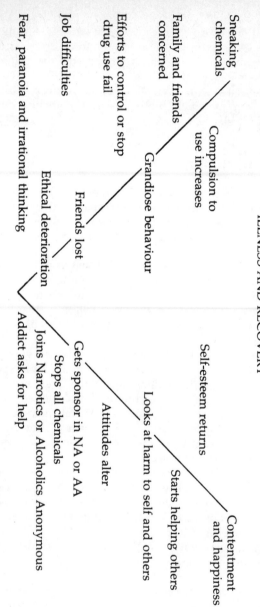

ILLNESS AND RECOVERY

Sneaking chemicals

Family and friends concerned

Compulsion to use increases

Efforts to control or stop drug use fail

Grandiose behaviour

Job difficulties

Friends lost

Ethical deterioration

Fear, paranoia and irrational thinking

Self-esteem returns

Starts helping others

Looks at harm to self and others

Attitudes alter

Gets sponsor in NA or AA

Stops all chemicals

Joins Narcotics or Alcoholics Anonymous

Addict asks for help

Contentment and happiness

8

Staying Off Drugs

The greatest danger facing a recovering addict or alcoholic is that of relapse. Chemical dependence is known as a 'relapsing illness'. Coming off drugs or drink is simple: staying off them is the real problem.

That is why no addict or alcoholic should think of himself or herself as cured. As we have said before, the addict is like a diabetic. To stay well a diabetic takes insulin daily, but is never cured of his diabetes.

In exactly the same way, there is no cure for chemical dependence, only a daily recovery, as long as the addict doesn't use drugs and the alcoholic doesn't drink. Once an addict or an alcoholic relapses into using drugs or drink again, the illness comes back with a vengeance.

Accepting that you cannot use

To become both sober and happy, you will have to accept right down at gut level that you cannot use mood-altering drugs of any kind. This means accepting the fact that even the smallest, tiniest amount of the drug or drink brings back the active phase of the illness.

The first sign of a relapse usually occurs in the addict's thinking.

The thinking precedes the using of drugs. Sometimes relapse occurs because the person fears rejection if he does not accept a drink or a drug. Or the addict or alcoholic becomes complacent, arrogant and starts to think: 'Damn the consequences.'

Often the thinking centres around the idea that somehow this time it will be different: this time the addict will somehow be able to control his drug-using, this time the alcoholic will be able to drink like an ordinary social drinker.

It is significant that the Narcotics Anonymous programme talks of an addict being 'powerless' over the addiction. It's not a familiar word to newcomers, and you may wonder how it applies to you.

Sometimes when an addict has been clean for a few days, subtle thoughts about using again begin to grow. 'I have proved I am not addicted, because I have given it up,' you may think. (That addicted mind of yours is getting pretty sneaky.)

Or the thought will come, 'I was only addicted to heroin. Pot won't hurt me. I can handle that.' Or the thought, 'A single glass of beer wouldn't hurt me.' Or even, 'Well, just one fix can't do any harm. I certainly won't have more than one.' (That addicted mind of yours is clearly desperate to think of an excuse.)

This is where the idea of powerlessness can be a help to you. Any addict or alcoholic can give up drugs or booze altogether. What they cannot do is control their drug-taking or drinking. For addicts and alcoholics it is either abstinence or excess. Moderation is something they cannot handle. It's just like the heavy cigarette smoker. He cannot cut down for any length of time. He has to choose between smoking like a train or giving up cigarettes altogether.

One way of seeing how powerless you were over drugs or drink is to write down ten examples of damage the drug or drink did to you. What did it do to your relationships, to your finances, to your working life, to your health, and (most of all) what did it do to your behaviour?

Now look at those ten examples. Did you *want* these things to happen? Of course you didn't. Basically you are not a bad person. You behaved badly because you were ill. These things happened because you went on taking drugs or drinking. And you went on taking drugs or drinking because you had to, because you were addicted.

That's powerlessness in action. And that's why you can't afford to take just one pill or fix or snort or drink.

The dangers of relapse

As we've said, the thoughts of using drugs come first; the actual drug-using then follows.

Use just one drug, take just one drink and it will all come back. Just one small pill or sniff or fix and it will activate the irrational thinking that leads inevitably back to using drugs or drinking. Once again it starts gnawing in the back of your mind. The emotional disorder will come right back into your head, and the crazy thinking will start up again.

And it won't stop there. You will relapse back into the illness's active phase and maybe suffer for years. You cannot count on being able to stop again. Any longstanding NA or AA member can tell tales of an addict or an alcoholic who had a relapse and whose funeral they attended. You may well have another drink or drug in you, but you may not have another recovery.

It doesn't matter how long you've been clean and sober. The illness is lying dormant within you and it can be activated after twenty years of sober, clean living by just one more fix or joint or drink.

Alas, you don't start again at the beginning of your drug-using or drinking. Many times it starts from the point at which you left off. It may even be worse after that length of time, as if while it lay dormant it progressed.

'At one point during my using, before I knew about NA, I managed to put down heroin and I stayed off it,' recalls William, a recovering addict who has now been in NA for three years. 'I wasn't clean. I was smoking dope, doing coke at parties, and drinking, so it was inevitable that I was going to go back and use heroin again. And when I did start again, it was as if time had telescoped, as if it was only twenty-four hours since I last used. I was straight back where I had been.'

You don't have to take what we say on trust. You can see for yourself by staying clean in NA or AA and watching others. They will demonstrate the truth of this for you. You will see what happens when they relapse. They do not come back to NA boasting of the good time they had. If they manage to make it back, they will tell tales of how this time it was worse than ever.

If you don't quite believe this, and you want to test it out here and now, ask around NAs at the next meeting till you find some-body who has had a relapse. They will tell you what happened.

Luckily, you don't have to learn this sad truth by personal experience. You can let others demonstrate it for you, and you can learn from their experience.

They are living proof of the dangers of relapse. Once you have seen it demonstrated in front of your eyes, you will know why you must put effort not just into stopping but into staying stopped.

Altering attitudes

If you want to stay clean, you will eventually find that you have to change the way you live – because the way a drug-using addict lives is not a good way for a recovering addict to live. In exactly the same way, a drinker's lifestyle is no good for a recovering alcoholic.

One of the secrets of staying stopped is to alter your attitudes about things. Indeed, AA members say that the initials of their fellowship stand not just for Alcoholics Anonymous but for Altered Attitudes. In the same way, NA could stand for New Attitudes. If you think about it, you will see it makes sense. In fact, if you are successfully staying off drugs and drink you are probably already practising this in small ways.

For example, you are probably already changing the way you think about drugs and drink. Instead of thinking about the pleasures of drug-taking or drinking, you are thinking about the bad times. You have altered your attitude towards drugs or drink and that new attitude is helping you stay away from them.

But this is just the beginning. There are many other attitudes which in the long run are going to need changing. Using drugs has affected your life and the way you think and feel in all kinds of ways. You may not yet know the full extent of what your addiction has done to you.

Characteristics of the using addict

For many years doctors and psychiatrists have been treating and studying addicts and alcoholics. As we have said before, they have come to the conclusion that chemical dependence is not just a physical illness; it is also an emotional illness.

They have detected a whole set of characteristics which are typical of drug-using addicts and drinking alcoholics. These characteristics are not at all pleasant.

1. *Drug-using addicts and drinking alcoholics are arrogant.* They have a big ego, coupled with a low sense of self-worth. They are full of

stubborn pride, yet at the same time they hate themselves. This arrogance makes them feel they know better than others. Often it stops them learning anything at all. A person who already knows everything is literally unteachable.

2. *Drug-using addicts and drinking alcoholics are over-sensitive.* They literally cannot bear criticism. And because they won't listen to criticism, they are unable to learn what is wrong with them. They are exquisitely sensitive to self, and almost completely insensitive to others. They always think of their own feelings, never of anybody else's. This self-obsession is part of the illness.

3. *Drug-using addicts and drinking alcoholics are full of self-pity.* They pity themselves. Oh, how they feel sorry for themselves! They feel that life has treated them badly. 'It's unfair,' is their complaint. 'Why should it happen to me?' is another cry. Drug-using addicts don't recognise that this is self-pity. They usually call it depression, which sounds much nicer.

4. *Drug-using addicts and drinking alcoholics can't bear frustration.* They cannot bear it when things don't work out their way. Addicts have very little control over their emotions and are likely to throw childish fits of rage if they are thwarted in any way. It's like a baby in the cot who drops his rattle – and sets up a howl immediately. When an addict wants something, he or she wants it **NOW**: instant results. Impatience is the other part of this characteristic.

5. *Drug-using addicts and drinking alcoholics are angry.* We have mentioned before the inner anger that afflicts using addicts. This anger permeates their whole life, and is quite unreasonable. They are angry at people, places and things. They are always blaming others and using this as an excuse not to do something about themselves. They often hide this anger from others so that it seems a kind of 'smiling anger'. In many cases they themselves do not know just how angry they are inside.

6. *Drug-using addicts and drinking alcoholics are unable to face reality.* Addicts find it hard to adapt to the real world as it is. They are not good at bearing the ordinary pain of life – indeed they take drugs to blot it out. They won't face unpleasant facts They prefer to ignore them, or even to deny them outright. Accepting things as they are is something they find very difficult indeed.

7. *Drug-using addicts and drinking alcoholics are frightened.* Addicts are not the blustering big egos they seem. Underneath they are fearful and, when it comes to the point of facing getting off drugs,

they are absolutely terrified. Paranoia is another symptom of their illness. They are frightened of people and have lost the ability to trust them. Their anger is often a cover-up for this fear. Many addicts say it is like being in a long dark tunnel with no light at the end.

8. *Drug-using addicts and drinking alcoholics are dishonest.* Addicts lie to themselves and to others all the time. They lie about their drug-using and its consequences, and they lie in other ways in order to go on using. This dishonesty becomes ingrained in all they do. Drug-using addicts may use constant small and quite unnecessary lies almost all the time. Worst of all they cannot be honest to themselves.

Healthier personality traits

For an addict to get well, these characteristics have to be replaced by healthier personality traits:

- arrogance must be replaced with humility;
- over-sensitivity with consideration for others' needs;
- self-pity with gratitude;
- inability to stand frustration with patience and emotional control;
- anger with caring;
- inability to face reality with acceptance of what really is;
- fear with trust;
- dishonesty with honesty.

As you read this book, you may feel that the words we are using are rather a turn-off. Words like 'humility', for instance, sound rather like something out of Sunday School.

Don't let these feelings of dismay blind you to what we are saying. Take 'humility' as an example. It has nothing to do with Uriah Heep-like grovelling. A person who is humble is somebody who is able to see that he or she is not perfect and is able to admit to mistakes. Therefore the humble person is able to learn from those same mistakes. Put like this, there really isn't anything wrong with the trait of 'humility'. It is just a question of adapting to the reality of what you are actually like.

But how on earth is the addict, just off drugs and still feeling upset, confused and probably rather ill, going to do all this? How can an alcoholic just a few days away from a drink change himself?

The Twelve Steps

This is where NA will help you. NA and AA have a recovery programme of Twelve Steps. These have been worked out from the experience of recovering addicts and alcoholics in the past half-century or so.

By following these steps, they discovered that they were able to stay away from drugs and drink not just for the odd day or week, but for years at a time. And, better still, by practising these steps they discovered how to be happy without drink or drugs.

For the aim of the Twelve Steps is nothing less than happiness. After all, someone who stays off drugs and drink but is miserably unhappy is in a very risky state of mind. Continuing unhappiness will make him or her wonder whether it wouldn't be better just to go back to drugs.

Addicts are not bad people trying to become good. They are sick people trying to get well. And the Twelve Steps of NA and AA are the method by which hundreds of thousands of addicts and alcoholics have recovered their emotional health and their personal dignity.

The Twelve Steps

1. We admitted we were powerless over alcohol, and that our lives had become unmanageable.

2. Came to believe that a Power greater than ourselves could restore us to sanity.

3. Made a decision to turn our will and our lives over to the care of God *as we understood Him.*

4. Made a searching and fearless moral inventory of ourselves.

5. Admitted to God, to ourselves, and to another human being the exact nature of our wrongs.

6. Were entirely ready to have God remove all these defects of character.

7. Humbly asked Him to remove our shortcomings.

8. Made a list of all persons we had harmed, and became willing to make amends to them all.

9. Made direct amends to such people whenever possible, except when to do so would injure them or others.

10. Continued to take personal inventory and when we were wrong promptly admitted it.

11. Sought through prayer and meditation to improve our conscious contact with God *as we understood Him*, praying only for knowledge of His will for us and the power to carry that out.

12. Having had a spiritual awakening as a result of these steps, we tried to carry this message to alcoholics and to practise these principles in all our affairs.

(Reprinted with permission of AA World Services Inc.)

In Narcotics Anonymous, these same steps are used as a programme of recovery. The only difference is that the word 'addict' is substituted for 'alcoholic' and the word 'addiction' for 'alcohol'.

Difficulties with the Twelve Steps

For many people coming to AA or NA for the first time, these steps seem an insuperable barrier. What on earth are they all about? What do they have to do with an illness?

It's worth remembering that, whatever you may think of them, these Twelve Steps *work*. They arose out of the experience of the first hundred alcoholics who got sober, and stayed sober, in the first year or so of AA. The Twelve Steps were not some moral formula dreamed up by outsiders. They were written down as a factual record of how those first hundred alcoholics recovered.

For those who find the Twelve Steps difficult to accept, we would like to offer an interpretation that might be helpful. We believe that the steps, exactly as they are, are a vital part of recovery for addicts and alcoholics. We think they encourage addicts and alcoholics to do the following:

1. Admit to the problem and to its effects on their lives.

2. Believe that NA or AA can help them get better.

3. Be willing to do what NA or AA suggest.

4. Get honest with themselves about the things they did when using drugs or drinking.

5. Get honest with somebody else about it – usually the NA or AA sponsor.

6. Readily admit that faulty attitudes need changing.

7. Be ready to co-operate with NA or AA in changing the attitudes.

8. List the harm caused to others by their drug-using or drinking.

9. Try to put that right, where possible.

10. Get into the habit of being honest to themselves, and admitting mistakes.

11. Be willing to accept that they are not the centre of the universe and that there are greater forces in the world.

12. Help other addicts recover and lead a healthy life with new and better values.

Because the Twelve Steps have this effect on addicts, it is important that they should be put into practice. You don't have to do them all at once. They are numbered in order. Start with number one, and then work your way through them. There is no deadline. Most people spend several weeks on the first step before starting the others.

And the best way to do them is to find a friend to guide you through them. That friend will normally be your NA or AA sponsor.

Getting a sponsor

When you have been to NA or AA meetings regularly for a number of weeks, you start getting to know the other members. Just like any group of people, you will find some you like very much, others you are less keen on.

Newcomers need a sponsor if they are to make proper progress towards recovery. The idea is to find a friend who has done what you are about to do, and who can therefore give you the benefit of support, comfort and advice.

Find somebody who has been in NA for at least a year or in AA for two years, and who has been completely clean and sober during that period. A member who has had periods back on drugs or drink is somebody who is clearly having difficulty with the programme of recovery. For a sponsor, you need somebody who is practising the programme successfully.

Normally, a sponsor should be of the same sex: women addicts should have a woman sponsor, men addicts a male sponsor. The idea is to avoid emotional and sexual entanglements. If the relationship works well, you will find yourself getting very close to your sponsor – which could lead to a love affair if you are not of the same sex.

Of course, gay men and women may want to have sponsors of the opposite sex, in order to avoid this possibility. The guiding principle is to choose a sponsor who will be a friend, not a lover.

Choose somebody you trust and like. It's no good having a sponsor whom you do not like, since this will make it much more difficult for you to confide in him or her. Sometimes people choose sponsors who have a similar background to themselves: at other times they choose sponsors who are quite different. Find somebody who works for you.

The greatest advantage in having a sponsor is in having somebody who knows all about you. Like a good long-lasting friend, you can talk out any difficulties with them, and they will know enough about you to know what is going on in your life.

At the beginning of your membership you may not know enough people to be sure of whom you want as a sponsor. But you can always ask somebody to act as a temporary sponsor till you can make your choice.

In the first few months of being clean, all kinds of painful emotions surface for the newly recovering addict. Living without drugs is not always easy, and sometimes daily life seems full of anxious moments or difficult situations. Having a friend to confide these things to makes them much easier to live through.

A sponsor is there to be *used*. Ideally, it should be somebody whom you see reasonably regularly in the course of your meetings. Regular telephone contact is also important. A sponsor you neither see nor telephone cannot help you properly, and, of course, *it is up to you to ask for the help you need*.

Getting involved in NA or AA

Most newly recovering addicts need to establish a routine of regular NA or AA meetings, where they see people they know and where other members get to know them. This not only makes for friendship, but also acts as a kind of check on the mental side of recovery. Longer-established members who get to know you will notice if you are going through a bad time or showing signs of dangerous thinking. They can help you with this.

Just going to meetings is probably all you can manage in the first few days and weeks of recovery. But as you begin to feel better, you will need to do a little bit more if you are to get the full benefit of recovery in NA or AA. Getting involved by doing some of the small tasks that make such meetings possible will help you recover. One of the most important things for an addict is to begin to change from a life of self-obsession towards a life of outgoing helpfulness to others.

'Five months after coming to the fellowship I started making the teas at a meeeting. The interesting thing was that at that time I was paralysingly shy. I found I couldn't talk to anyone. I couldn't hold proper conversations. I could only issue random statements. I had to re-learn how to do it,' recalls Alison, a recovering addict and alcoholic who has been clean and sober for eight years. 'Making the tea helped. One day I was pouring the tea and the meeting secretary came up to me and said: "Will you be nice to Jenny? She's terribly shy."

'I said to him, "But I'm terribly shy too."

' "You're less shy than she is," he said. So I made a monumental effort to overcome my shyness. And in the future, that was how I coped. When I was feeling shy I looked for someone even more shy than I was. Doing the teas at a meeting taught me how to talk again.'

Difficulties with NA or AA

Some people take to NA or AA without any difficulty at all. As soon as they walk into a meeting, they have a feeling of coming home. They are able immediately to grasp the friendship offered, and are quite happy to try to do what is suggested.

For others, just the opposite occurs. If you are one of the people who does not immediately enjoy the meetings, try to think of them as treatment for your illness. For instance, if you had cancer, you would accept chemotherapy for it even though such treatment is painful. It may help you to think of NA or AA in this way. OK, so for the time being you do not enjoy it. But that is not the point. Like medicine it is good for you whether you enjoy it or not. So keep going.

It will help if you go to several different meetings. The exact format of a meeting varies. Some are large with lots of people; others may have only half a dozen people and a much more intimate atmosphere. Going round several meetings allows you to find one at which you feel at home.

Many newcomers to NA and AA meetings are upset when they hear people talking about God. 'I used to be squirming every time the word "God" was mentioned,' recalls Alison. 'Then a member explained the difference between spiritual and religious.'

This reaction to the way God is mentioned in the NA or AA Twelve Steps and in the prayer is quite common. Sometimes believers are just as horrified as unbelievers. Yet, if they just keep going to the meetings, they will discover that the membership includes many people who, like them, were initially worried by the idea of God.

A belief in God is not necessary for belonging to NA or AA.

Atheists can recover in the Twelve-Step programme just as well as believers. What is important is to get out of the driving seat, *to stop doing it your way.*

Spiritual not religious

It is important to realise that the programme of recovery in NA is not a religious one. You do not have to have any religious belief whatsoever in order to practise it.

But it is a *spiritual* programme. It is designed to help your spirit, the inner you, to recover from the harm addiction has done to it. Chemical dependence is a threefold illness: it harms the body, it harms the mind, and it harms the spirit of the addict.

Exactly how you interpret 'spiritual' is up to you. Some people think of it as what concerns the ethical part of a human being. Others think of it as the soul. Some people think of it as applying to the conscience in themselves. Still others are happy with the idea of an inward spirit. You are free to interpret things as you choose in NA.

In the same way, you can give the word 'God' whatever meaning you choose. Some people add an extra 'o' to the word, and think of it as 'Good'. Others concentrate on the idea that they cannot recover from chemical dependence on their own, and so they need a Higher Power of some kind.

This Higher Power can be the collective power of the group (stronger than any individual's strength), or the philosophy of AA and NA, or the Twelve Steps of recovery. Once again, an individual is free to choose whatever interpretation will help him or her to get well.

Those with a lot of intellectual pride sometimes find this difficult. They are so used to using brain power to solve all their problems that they have a tendency to think themselves out of NA and AA. This keeps them sick. If you are plagued with intellectual doubts, use your brain to think yourself *into* NA or AA. That way you will get well.

Doing it your way

Some addicts have an overwhelming confidence that their way of getting clean is better than anybody else's. They may be unwilling to follow the suggestions of NA and AA, or unwilling even to consider them.

This problem of unwillingness in less extreme ways afflicts many addicts just off drugs and alcoholics just off drink. It is part of the way the sick mind tries to make excuses to get back to the drug it craves.

This is where will power can help you get well. If you feel unwilling to do the things suggested, use your will power to do them even though you do not want to. *Make* yourself go to meetings, however much you loathe them. *Make* yourself listen and at least consider the suggestions made to you.

The brutal truth is that you are 99 per cent likely to be wrong. Addicts who are still using drugs, or who are only a few weeks off them, still have minds and hearts which are distorted by drugs. A drinking alcoholic, or one who has only just stopped drinking, cannot think clearly. They do not know better than those who have been clean and sober for months and years.

Look at it this way. For years you have been doing it your way. And what was your way? It was a lifestyle that involved using drugs. Doing it your way made you ill with chemical dependence, and kept you ill for years.

Do you really want it all back? For if you do things your way, you will go back to using drugs or to drinking.

You don't have to do it all at once

If you are one of the unwilling ones, concentrate on getting to meetings, getting involved and getting a sponsor to help you through the daily difficulties. If God and the Twelve Steps make you worried, you can shelve them for the first few weeks.

Regular attendance at meetings and keeping clear of drugs are the essentials. Practise doing the little things that people suggest, because many of the small practical suggestions of how to stay away from drugs, how to deal with drinking situations, what to do about old using and abusing friends, and so forth are easy to accept.

You will notice that recovering addicts often do not give advice directly. Instead they talk about what *they* did, and what parts of the programme worked for them. It's impossible to take offence at this. After all, they are only reporting the facts.

The facts of their experience can help you, if you let them. Of course everybody is different, and what works for one individual may not work for another if circumstances are very different. For instance, the experience of a single person may not be able to help others with their marriage problems.

But when people have the same kind of trouble, then usually the experience of a longstanding member will have something that you can learn from it. A married member will be able to tell you about the strain on his marriage during the first few weeks of recovery. If you are undergoing the same strain, you will probably be able to learn something from his experience.

The other mental trick that sometimes helps unwilling people do what is suggested is to use the 24-hour plan. Just for one day you might be willing to do something which otherwise you would reject. Looked at in this way, you do not need quite as much willingness.

Trust in NA and AA

Getting clean and sober is rather like a leap in the dark. You are bound to be dismayed and frightened about the future. You are at the beginning of a big change in life. And in the first few weeks you may well have fears and doubts about it.

Trust in NA and AA. Of course, the future seems scary at the moment, but when so many addicts have stayed clean thanks to doing what the programme suggests, it is overwhelmingly likely that it will work for you too. Remind yourself of all the happy recovering addicts who used to feel like you do but who are now making it. All you have to do is give it a try today.

Unwillingness can and does change to willingness, just as long as newcomers are in close contact with NA or AA. As long as you stay away from drugs or drink and keep going to the meetings, you will recover.

9

Recovery: a Healthy Body

Both alcohol and drugs can damage the body as well as the mind and the emotions. But physically most young addicts and alcoholics recover very quickly, even when their drug-use has been severe. Older addicts and alcoholics may face a longer period of physical recovery.

For most people, it is a good idea to get back to normal living as soon as possible. An active and fulfilled life is far better protection against relapse than a life empty of interests.

Taking care of the body by getting proper food, rest and recreation is part of recovery. Drug-using addicts are quite often impervious to their body's needs, failing to eat and to take proper rest. If you still fail to do this now that you are clean, it's clear that you have not altered your attitudes sufficiently.

So eat proper meals, with plenty of fresh fruit and vegetables. Give yourself enough rest. The mind and body are inter-connected. If your body is unwell, it will translate that unwellness to your mind and you will probably start feeling depressed or over-anxious.

It's just like running a car. If you never have it serviced or properly maintained, you are increasing your chance of a breakdown. In the same way, regular petrol and oil are needed, otherwise it will just stop going.

Exercise and relaxation

Many addicts and alcoholics have difficulty in relaxing in the first months of their recovery. For years they have sedated their bodies with drugs and alcohol, and when these are no longer available they find it difficult to use natural methods of relaxation. Tranquilliser addicts in particular suffer from the inability to relax.

Exercise is probably the best natural method of ensuring relaxation. A healthy body, which is tired out by exercises, relaxes naturally. Sleep often comes easily at the end of a day which has included some physical activity.

Be sensible. Tranquilliser addicts need to take extra care not to overdo things in the first weeks of coming off the drug. Tranquillisers are a muscle relaxant, and the muscles take time to adjust to a drug-free body. Heavy effort or violent exercise can easily send the muscles into painful spasm in the first few weeks. All exercise should be started gently, and gradually worked up.

As well as jogging, tennis and other games, many people enjoy gymnasium work-outs and aerobic dancing. Gymnasiums and health clubs often have saunas, massage and Jacuzzis, which will help you unwind. Then there are the familiar activities of biking, marathon running, gardening or riding. Swimming seems particularly effective in promoting relaxation.

Various organisations put out relaxation tapes, which are worth trying. In some communities there are group relaxation or exercise classes. Yoga classes may help too. You will find some helpful addresses in Appendix 3.

Women and health

Heavy drug users often find that they have ceased to menstruate. When this happens, it may be several months before periods start up again. And when they do return, they may be irregular, scanty or excessive. If you are worried, see your doctor and sort it out with him. But, as a rough guide, it may take your body up to a year to get its gynaecological functions back to normal.

Incidentally, period pains seem much more severe once you are clean and sober. It is difficult to know whether this means they really are worse, or simply that they *seem* worse. After years of living under drugged sedation, it can be quite a surprise to feel any kind of ordinary pain! Besides, addicts and alcoholics in the early stages of recovery are bad at enduring any kind of pain or discomfort.

Sex and drug-using

Initially, some drugs are sexually stimulating; others tend to decrease sexuality. Drink, as the drunken porter in *Macbeth* said, 'provokes the desire, but it takes away the performance'.

Many addicts and alcoholics have lived distorted sex lives under the influence of drugs and alcohol. When they come clean and sober up, it usually takes some time for this side of their life to settle down. Time is needed to heal the emotional wounds and to sort out their sexual lives.

'Drinking was always associated with sex and I always had rather unsatisfactory, rather torrid relationships. It seemed to me that sex was a parallel appetite to booze,' says a recovering alcoholic and addict who has been clean and sober for about five years.

In addiction, drugs and drink distort sexual behaviour. Some women are sexually abused while under the influence of drink or drugs. Others turn to a sexually promiscuous lifestyle. Some women addicts or alcoholics turn to prostitution and some male addicts, including those who are heterosexual, turn to homosexual prostitution to support their using. Sexual infections and subsequent visits to VD clinics are a common part of this drugs or drink lifestyle.

Compulsive sex sometimes accompanies compulsive drug-use. Men, too, sometimes participate in sexual acts that they would not have taken part in if they had been clean and sober. When they get clean it is quite common for addicts and alcoholics to feel a lot of guilt and remorse about this part of their drug-using life and to feel very awkward at initiating any kind of relationship. They have to relearn intimacy.

Getting rid of the past

In both AA and NA there is a way to deal with sexual guilt from the past. Both organisations suggest that addicts and alcoholics should make a kind of inventory of their destructive behaviour and then talk it over with a trusted person – their sponsor, a minister or priest, or a therapist. This is taking the fourth and fifth steps in the AA and NA programme of recovery.

The advantage of following this tested advice is that it draws a line under the past. Often the temptation is to smother the past, to try to bury it beyond recall. This does not work. Dealing with feelings is the only way. The way to emotional recovery is to face and accept all the horrors of the past, and then put them behind you. It takes courage to do this and yet it is a vital part of getting well. Guilt and anxiety fade away through putting the fourth and fifth steps into action.

It is not usually a good idea, however, to confess everything to a partner. You will be unloading your own guilt at the expense of their peace of mind. In the same way, detailed talk about the sexual past is often best kept between newcomer and sponsor, rather than spoken of at meetings where it can sometimes disturb members who are still not well.

Sex in recovery

Most addicts feel considerable anxiety about sex now that they are clean and sober. Many of them have literally never had sex without having also had some mood-altering drug or drink. Completely sober sex is thus a new experience which frightens many. Many male addicts will have been impotent at times during their drug-using and drinking life. Because of drug or drink use, many women will have had few, if any, orgasms.

If you are single, it is not a good idea to rush into a sexual relationship. Newly recovering addicts find the emotional side of a love affair just too difficult to handle. They find themselves heading for disaster. In some way, addicts and alcoholics only a few months off drugs or drink are like teenagers. They become passionately infatuated very easily. When the love affair breaks up – as such infatuations usually do – the pain of it is almost unbearable.

Newly recovering alcoholics and addicts should avoid relationships in their first year of recovery. This is nothing to do with puritanism. It is simply that the drama and pain of a love affair are too much for them. Rushing into love affairs too soon may result in turning back to drinking or drug-using.

It is also a good idea not to get involved with other recovering addicts or alcoholics of the opposite sex in the first year of recovery. Really well-balanced addicts who have been clean for several years don't pick up or get emotionally involved with newcomers. Those who do tend to be the less healthy members and should be avoided for that very reason. You don't want a sick relationship on your hands!

Apart from anything else, keeping away from relationships for the first year helps you concentrate on recovery. And in the first year this is, above everything else, where all your energies should be centered.

Getting comfortable with sex

Many addicts and alcoholics take time to become comfortable with sex. Those who are married or have partners may find themselves making love without any mood-altering drink or drugs virtually for the first time. Shyness and embarrassment are common.

Often they are frightened of sex, particularly if demeaning sex was part of their drug-using or drinking life. In reaction to this, recovering addicts and alcoholics sometimes become unnecessarily puritanical about lovemaking. They may associate certain sexual acts with using drugs.

Partners are not always enthusiastic about resuming a sex life that in the past was damaged by drugs or drink. Many partners have been deeply wounded by the experience of living with a drug-using addict or a drinking alcoholic. It may be months before they can trust again – and good lovemaking usually needs emotional trust.

Recovering addicts and alcoholics have to learn that the ability to screw has nothing to do with lovemaking. Sexual love requires not just bedroom gymnastics but kindness, care, control and emotional generosity. These qualities are usually conspicuously absent in drug users and alcoholic drinkers. Yet it is these qualities that will please a partner and make lovemaking into what it should be. The earth need not always move. Sometimes lovemaking is a question of cuddling, comfort and warmth, or just fun rather than ecstasy.

Women addicts sometimes need to learn to be assertive rather than passive in their sexual lives. If you do not dare ask for what you want, you may feel resentment that your partner did not do it. Making your needs clear will help you to a healthy sex life.

In the same way, you are entitled to say 'No'. This two-letter word is nothing to be afraid of. Now that you are recovering from the illness of addiction, you have regained the right to do only what you feel is good for you. You and your body deserve respect.

Masturbation is another sexual activity which often worries recovering addicts and alcoholics, both male and female. In the first year of recovery, when an addict is trying to stay away from emotional relationships, masturbation may be a natural sexual resource which can help sexual frustration.

Gay men and women

Recovery involves getting honest in all areas of your life. Many gay women and men have found it hard to come to terms with their homosexuality, and have tried to live as heterosexuals. The disordered sex lives so common in addicts may mean that they have been untrue to their real selves, taking refuge in an insincere heterosexuality. Other gay men and women have taken up a 'cruising-and-using' lifestyle.

Often, becoming clean and sober prompts them to accept their homosexuality for the first time. In big cities there are sometimes gay Alcoholics Anonymous meetings. In ordinary meetings there are many clean and sober gay men and women who will help those who are coming to terms with their sexuality.

Getting extra help

Sometimes recovering addicts remain unhappy with their sexuality. Sexual compulsiveness and sexual obsession do not always die away when the drugs or drink are put down. They may persist into recovery.

The Twelve-Step programme of NA and AA can be used to deal with sexual addiction problems. So can the 24-hour plan of staying away from something for just one day. The house-cleaning involved in the fourth and fifth steps of the AA and NA programme helps immeasurably.

If these measures are not enough, you may need extra help from a therapist. Ask around NA or AA friends to see if they can recommend a therapist who knows about the Twelve-Step programme. If not, there are organisations listed in Appendix 3 which could help.

Any major sexual difficulties between partners can also be tackled by counselling. Bringing these into the open, with the help of a trained counsellor, often diminishes them or does away with them altogether. Indeed, all important sexual anxieties are probably best brought into the open in this way. Some addicts have been the victims of incest in their past. Facing this with a counsellor will mean that the past begins to lose its power to hurt or frighten you. Appendix 3 has the addresses of many different organisations which deal with this and other relationship difficulties.

Finding a partner

Most young and single people probably want to find a partner they can live with in a loving relationship. And there is absolutely no reason why recovering addicts and alcoholics, once they have developed some emotional balance, should not love others, marry them and have children.

This will probably involve re-learning the places of getting acquainted, because recovering addicts and alcoholics are not usually at ease in drinking spots like pubs and clubs. Yet there are other places where boys meet girls. There are swimming pools, dances, beaches, holidays, evening classes, offices, launderettes, restaurants, concerts (pop and classical), libraries, church and synagogue groups. But the most obvious place to meet people is at work.

How to make contact with strangers is something most young people learn in their teenage years. Those who have turned to drugs may never have learned this. So be prepared to feel a little shyness as you begin to lead a normal social life.

'The first time I made a date in sobriety, I worried about it for days beforehand – what I should wear, what I should do, whether I could kiss her,' says Michael, a thirty-eight-year-old recovering alcoholic with three years' sobriety. 'I was full of panic. Imagine it! Worrying about a little kiss. I had screwed my way round the world in my drinking, but now I was full of anxiety about a date!'

Of course, you will also meet others at NA and AA meetings, and many NAs or AAs do marry each other successfully. However, it is risky taking up with an addict or an alcoholic who has been continuously clean and sober for less than two years. You might find yourself involved with a drug-using addict or a drinking alcoholic – and that will be no fun at all.

Some addiction counsellors take the view that even clean and sober addicts should think carefully about marrying each other and having their own children. As addiction seems to be passed on genetically, they may be giving their children a double dose of the addiction gene.

Sometimes the search for a partner becomes an obsession. 'If only I can find the right person, then all my troubles will be over . . .' thinks the addict. They are hunting for a partner to solve their problems, just as they used drugs to do so.

This kind of substitution is an extraordinarily bad start to any relationship and is likely to end in unhappiness. It is important to remember that depending on any person for your happiness is unhealthy – no matter how reliable, kind and competent that person is. Only when you can live happily alone, and your self-worth comes from within, are you fit to live happily with another.

Addicts and illness

On the whole, recovering addicts are a healthy bunch once they have been a year or more away from drugs. Nevertheless, if they do become ill, many of them worry about what drugs and medicines they should take.

The guiding rule is: only take drugs which are legitimately prescribed for a real illness by a doctor who knows about addiction. All addicts and alcoholics should explain their history of addiction to any doctor or dentist who is treating them. They should also tell any hospital authorities that need to know. For instance, addicts and alcoholics usually need larger doses of anaesthesia.

Be specific about what drugs you were using, and how long you have been clean and sober. Tell the doctor that you need to avoid any mood-altering drugs because as a recovering addict or alcoholic you are likely to become addicted to them.

This means keeping away from all tranquillisers and sleeping pills, which doctors sometimes prescribe quite freely. Given to ordinary people in small doses, these drugs are harmless. But for addicts or alcoholics they are a serious problem. It is better to remain temporarily sleepless and anxious than to take the benzodiazepine drugs.

A complete list of these and other sedative drugs can be found in Appendix 1. You should also stay away from cough medicines, kaolin–morphine mixtures, and any patent medicines which contain codeine, paracetamol, alcohol and morphine. Always check exactly what patent medicines contain before buying them.

If taking any liquid medicine, check with the chemist whether it has an alcohol base. Many liquid medicines do. Stick to aspirins (soluble and otherwise) as painkillers. If you are prescribed painkillers in hospital after an operation, don't take them home with you afterwards. If there is a legitimate medical condition for which you need painkillers, take the minimum. Collect small prescriptions regularly rather than one large prescription for several weeks.

Unfortunately, not all doctors understand addiction. Quite unknowingly, some will prescribe unsuitable medicines even though you have told them that you are a recovering addict or alcoholic.

Alison discovered when she asked her family doctor about migraine that he didn't understand about addiction. 'He gave me DF 118, which I later discovered was a synthetic narcotic. I didn't know what it was. I took half the dose and felt really spaced out. So I threw away the pills and now I only use aspirin, and not too much of that.'

If you have this kind of trouble with a doctor, it may be worth changing to a different practice. Most family doctors are only too delighted when an addict or an alcoholic becomes clean and sober. But there remain some who simply don't understand chemical dependence, and who thus may be irritated with addicts trying to avoid mood-altering drugs. It is probably best to change doctors rather than stay with a doctor who does not understand your illness. Local NA or AA members will know of sympathetic practitioners.

Make use of drug-free alternatives to traditional medicine, if you think they will help. A list of alternative-medicine organisations can be found in Appendix 3. Avoid therapies that are run by religious cults, pushed by high-pressure sales techniques, or which charge unreasonably high fees. Faddish or extreme diets should be avoided too.

Just like ordinary people, recovering addicts and alcoholics sometimes develop other emotional disorders which require help. Get help from a counsellor or therapist who understands chemical dependence and alcoholism, so that your underlying difficulties can be tackled. It is always better to try to talk your problems away first, rather than medicate them away. You will find other NA and AA members know of therapists they have found useful. Ask around the meetings.

Insomnia

Insomnia is one of the commonest side-effects of withdrawal from drugs and alcohol, so you must expect some sleepless nights in the first few months of coming off drugs.

Although people never die from lack of sleep, wakeful nights are very wearing on the nerves. Usually the person lies in bed worrying about not sleeping, or paces around the flat trying to think up some activity to while away the hours.

Getting through a sleepless night will be easier if you try to remain in bed. This maximises your chances of eventually sleeping. After all, nobody sleeps in the vertical position, so stay horizontal! A bedside light and a pleasant but dull book will help while away the hours. Some people find that this is a good time to re-read NA or AA literature to calm the mind. A cup of hot milk or malted milk sometimes helps.

If you are more than six months off drugs and you are still not sleeping well, it is worth taking measures to deal with your insomnia. As a first step, keep a diary to see if there is any pattern to your sleeplessness.

For some women insomnia is linked to hormonal changes in the body. Just knowing this makes it easier to bear, for there is also the comfort of knowing that as the difficult days pass the period of sleeplessness will come to an end.

Here are some of the measures you can take to deal with insomnia:

1. Follow a fixed routine. If you don't get up till noon, it is foolish to expect your body to fall asleep by midnight. A chaotic lifestyle of late mornings and late nights, with no set pattern of sleeping and waking, will make sleep that much more difficult. Get up at a normal hour, no matter how sleepless the preceding night was. Try to develop a routine of waking and sleeping which will give the body regular hours.

2. Go to bed earlier. Some people cannot fall asleep until late because they have not allowed long enough to wind down in the evening. Many people need half an hour or an hour to wind themselves down at the end of the day – pottering about, brushing their teeth and generally moving towards the bedroom.

If you are taking late-night phone calls, working till the late hours of the evening, or generally staying active until the last minute, you may not be allowing a long enough wind-down period. So start moving towards bed a little earlier.

3. Avoid coffee, tea and all drinks containing caffeine after 6 p.m. It is worth remembering that cola and many other canned drinks have a huge caffeine content. Try malted milk or hot blackcurrant last thing at night.

4. Take physical exercise during the day. Some people make a routine of taking a swim or doing a gymnasium work-out after sedentary work. Physical tiredness, unlike emotional exhaustion, promotes healthy sleep.

5. Keep the bed warm. Hot-water bottles, bedsocks and electric blankets are not to be despised. Most bodies heat up just before slumber. If you make sure your body is warmed up, it may sleep more easily.

6. Try a meditation routine. Methods of relaxation, taught in

relaxation classes, can often be practised last thing at night in bed.

7. Ear plugs to cut down noise and eye masks to cut out the light also help some people.

Insomnia sometimes reflects the emotional well-being of people. Those who are severely depressed wake early in the morning. They need help for their depression, and then their insomnia will often diminish.

Likewise, those who are angry, anxious, or not at peace with themselves for whatever reason, may find it difficult to sleep. Getting to meetings, confiding your problems to your sponsor and trying to help others can put the mind at rest. A quiet mind is more likely to sleep well.

It must be admitted that some people probably have a naturally high level of alertness, and in them insomnia may persist whatever measures are taken. If this happens, acceptance is the answer. Try to get bed-rest in comfortable surroundings with a radio or a good book, even if you cannot sleep. If you sleep in a double bed, radios which have earplugs, and a small reading light won't interfere with your partner's rest. Partners will appreciate your thoughtfulness and be more sympathetic if you try not to disturb them.

10

Recovery: a Healthy Mind and Altered Attitudes

If you are going to be happy as well as free from drugs you will need to do a considerable amount of work on yourself. As we have said earlier, addicts who want to stay off drugs and live happy lives will have to alter many of their attitudes.

Let's look a little closer at this business of changing attitudes. It is at the heart of successful recovery. By now, if you have been clean for several weeks, the chances are that all kinds of feelings are coming back to you. Some of these feelings are pleasant – joy, laughter, caring. Others are extremely unpleasant. These are feelings like anger, jealousy, self-pity, depression and anxiety. Sometimes these feelings simmer away inside you and you are not even sure what they are.

Name them, own them, dump them

If you are feeling unhappy or restless or ill at ease, the first thing to do is to look at yourself and ask yourself: 'What is going on? What are my feelings at this moment?'

Identify the emotion. Is it anxiety? Perhaps things are not going right in your life and you are worrying about the future. Is it resentment? Are you going over something in your mind that makes you feel angry?

Now admit to yourself, 'Yes, that is what I am feeling.' One of the reasons why people stay very uncomfortable in themselves is that they don't admit to their feelings. Through clenched teeth they say things like 'Of course, I'm not angry *but . . .*'

Once you have admitted what it is that you are feeling, you can get rid of the uncomfortable feelings by talking about them at meetings, phoning your sponsor and in general getting them out into the open and dumping them.

But these measures, excellent though they are, are only temporary ones. In the long run, in order to lead a contented life, you must take action to prevent the negative feelings arising in the first place.

What makes people have bad feelings

Attitudes, your inner attitudes, produce bad feelings like fear, anger and anxiety.

'Nonsense!' you think. 'I am angry because my parents behave so unreasonably. And I'm jealous because my wife is up to something. As for my anxiety, who wouldn't be anxious about getting a job in a society where jobs are so hard for someone like me to find?'

Like most people, addicts and non-addicts, you probably feel that people, places and things cause your bad feelings. But this really isn't so. *It is your attitude to people, places and things which causes your bad feelings.*

Faulty attitudes cause your unhappiness

Now let's take an example. Let's say there are two recovering addicts, both in Narcotics Anonymous trying to get well, both still living at home with their respective parents.

Both sets of parents decide that it's time they had the house to themselves. They ask their addicts if they will find somewhere else to live and move out of the family home.

One addict takes this as a personal affront. His attitude is that it's not fair. Therefore he sulks and he storms and he is full of self-pity and resentment. Very soon, he goes back to using drugs.

The other addict's attitude is entirely different. He sees this as a good chance towards growing up in recovery. Instead of feeling sorry for himself, he feels pleased and rather excited by the idea of getting his own place, and sets about doing so with the help of his parents.

Exactly the same thing happened to each addict – they were both asked to leave home. But the attitude of one was that this was an unfair demand, while the attitude of the other was that this was a chance for growth. And because their attitudes were different, their emotional reactions were different too. One felt self-pity and anger, the other felt pleasure and excitement. One went back to using drugs; the other stayed clean.

The sequence of events goes like this. Something happens – you evaluate it according to your inner attitudes – you experience an emotional reaction.

You *make yourself feel bad*

It is your thinking that makes you unhappy. It is your mind and its attitudes that make you fearful, anxious, angry, jealous or full of self-pity. And it is these faulty attitudes that make you unhappy.

Let's look at another example. Suppose you decide that it's time in your recovery to get a job. You see a suitable one advertised. You write in for it and get an interview. But after a few days you get a letter saying that you are not getting the job.

Your emotional reaction is a negative one. You feel depressed and angry and worthless all at once.

Have a closer look at these feelings. What are the thoughts in your head? Here are some of the things your mind is saying: 'It's not fair. I'm doing all I can to recover from addiction, and now I get this kind of set-back. That firm have no right to do that sort of thing to me. The rejection might have made me go back to using. I'll never get a job at this rate. I am obviously worth nothing. I'm a hopeless, worthless human being.'

These negative thoughts are what are producing the anger, self-pity and bad feelings in you. What do they say about your inner attitudes?

Well, one of your attitudes is obviously that: 'I am owed special favours because I gave up using drugs.' Another attitude, and this is a dangerous one, is: 'If things don't go the way I want them to, I can use drugs again.' And here's another: 'If at first I don't succeed, it means I never will get anywhere.' And here's a real downer attitude: 'Not getting this job means I am a bad, worthless, hopeless human being.'

All these attitudes are irrational. There's nothing in the order of the universe which says that recovering addicts are entitled to special treatment. Indeed, there's nothing in the universe which says life's joys and problems are going to be distributed fairly to anybody. Fairness doesn't come into it.

It's also irrational to let yourself think that if things don't go the way you want them, then you can use drugs. Who will suffer from that? Not the firm who failed to hire you. *You* will suffer.

Finally, the healthy attitude to disappointment is one that gets on with trying, as in the motto: 'If at first you don't succeed, try, try and try again.' Being rejected for a job really says nothing about you as a human being. Maybe somebody better qualified turned up.

Changing attitudes

Changing your attitudes will make you happier. It really will. Setbacks like not getting a job you wanted won't leave you in a pit of self-pity, worthlessness and anger if you have the right attitude. With the right attitude to life, you will simply see if there's anything that can be learned from the experience, then shrug your shoulders and get on with the next job interview.

Here are some healthy attitudes that will help you lead a happier life.

1. *Accept that life isn't fair*. It isn't fair to anybody. If you think you are having a bad time, just think of somebody aged twenty in a terminal cancer ward. Remember, self-pity leads back to using drugs. Every time the thought 'It's unfair!' comes into your head, chase it out again. It's childish thinking.

2. *Set yourself realistic goals*. If you can't get what you want, start wanting what you can get. Part of recovery is learning to live with reality as it really is. And that means being realistic about yourself and what you can achieve. 'It's important to realise reality is reality *and not what you want it to be*,' says a counsellor who helps people think realistically.

3. *Allow yourself to make mistakes*. Every human being makes mistakes and, what's more, many of those mistakes are valuable experiences. Think it out for yourself. What do you learn from your successes? Not much. What do you learn from your mistakes? A great deal.

4. *Drop the words 'should', 'ought', 'must' from your thinking*. Reality simply doesn't recognise these words. When you start thinking thoughts with these words in them, have a closer look at them.

Why 'should', 'ought', 'must' you? Who says so? You? Think again. There's absolutely nothing in the universe which takes any notice of these 'should', 'ought', 'must' rules that you are imposing on yourself.

Sometimes they run absolutely counter to what reality is, like 'I ought to love my mother but I don't.' Sometimes they just impose a burden on you, like 'I must get that job.' Reality isn't how you think it ought to be. All those planets, galaxies and worlds simply don't recognise one little addict's petty self-imposed rules. Remember: 'Reality is reality, *not what you want it to be.*'

5. *Stop 'awfulising'*. It's 'awful', 'terrible', 'disastrous', 'horrifying'. Really? Is it really awful compared with, say, millions of people dying from famine in Africa? Is it terrible compared with dying from leukaemia or lung cancer, or spending your life in a wheelchair? Is it disastrous compared with the havoc caused by an earthquake or a volcano? You know it isn't anything of the kind. Every time you exaggerate in your thinking like this, you make things worse. Bring yourself back to reality by trying to see things in their proper perspective.

6. *Let go of making yourself feel bad*. If you have a problem that is worrying or angering you, take a careful look at it. Identify exactly what you are allowing to bug you. If there's some action you can take today, take it. Then stop worrying or angering yourself about it and let the problem go.

Literally stop the thoughts. Worrying or getting angry about something you cannot change is simply a waste of thinking power. It clutters up your head with unwanted rubbish. Every time this kind of rubbish thought comes into your head, chase it out with something else. Take realistic actions and change your mental focus from the problem to something quite different.

You can help yourself let go of things by talking about them at a meeting, talking to your sponsor, handing them over in prayer. One recovering addict uses this mental trick. She takes the whatever is worrying her, imagines it being wrapped up in a paper parcel, then posts it into a kind of imaginary celestial letter box. Another recovering alcoholic simply finds a suffering newcomer to help, in order to stop being obsessive about her own problems. Ask around NA or AA and you'll find other people have ways of letting go which may help you.

7. *See things from other people's points of view*. Take yourself out of the centre of your myopic mental frame and look at things through their eyes. It's surprising what a different mental landscape you'll see.

Take the bus conductor who was rude to you today. Before you snap back, imagine what his day may have been like. He had a disagreement with his family at breakfast, arrived at the bus garage to find his shift altered, and has just had a row with somebody trying to evade the proper fare. So he was rude to you, but you weren't really his target. He'd have been rude to the next passenger whoever it was. So it's not worth taking so personally.

8. *Don't expect too much from others.* Just because people are not addicts or alcoholics does not mean that they are saints. The world is full of different kinds of people, and quite a few of them are emotionally immature. You can't expect rational responses from emotionally ill people.

9. *Don't let other people press your buttons.* You can choose your reactions to others in the same way that you can choose your attitudes. If somebody is angry to you, you need not be angry back. You do not have to pick up his anger.

Learning to care for others

Even for somebody trying their hardest to change their attitudes, some aspects of life remain difficult. It's sometimes quite easy to practise the principles of a new life in the world outside, but very difficult to practise them in the home.

The family and its relationships are often a persistent source of difficulty to recovering addicts. Most addicts come into NA or AA with their relationships in tatters. Drugs have come between them and friends, family and partners. Indeed, drugs have often destroyed their ability to express care for others.

As we have said, addicts prefer to get stoned in company, and sometimes drug users will even introduce their younger brothers and sisters to drugs. They only think of their own selfish needs and do not stop to think of the possible outcome.

It is little wonder, therefore, that by the time addicts reach NA or AA there is a trail of broken relationships and emotional damage to others in the past. Drug addiction harms not only the addicts, but also those around them. Indeed, specialists call drug dependence a family illness because of the emotional damage to all those around the addict or alcoholic.

Family reactions
Most families have been through a gamut of emotions as they

watched their loved one sinking into chemical dependence. They have suffered from despair, anger, frustration and guilt. Months, sometimes years, of pressure on the family have caused them to become emotionally damaged themselves.

If the family has joined Families Anonymous or Al-anon, they will recognise this damage to themselves and will be recovering while their addict recovers. They will be getting on with their own lives and they will understand what is happening to the addict.

Families who refuse to go to these organisations, however, may stay in almost total ignorance of the illness of chemical dependence. Just as they did not understand it when you were using drugs, so they do not understand your recovery.

They may greet the joyful news that you are in NA or AA and recovering a day at a time with downright disbelief or suspicious scepticism. You may find that they are still checking up on you or treating you as if you were still on drugs or still drinking.

Before you react with childish anger, think about it from their point of view. After all, they've heard your promises many times before. They've exhausted themselves hoping this really would be the last time you took drugs or drank. They've been through the despair of realising your promises weren't kept. They have listened to the innumerable lies you told them while you were using drugs or drinking.

Why should they believe you now? *You* know it's different this time, because *you* understand about NA and the programme, but *they* don't understand it. They may even be wildly suspicious of the idea that recovering addicts or alcoholics can help each other. Many people who have never gone to a public NA or AA meeting *are* suspicious.

If this is their attitude, stop trying to persuade, coax or bully them into understanding. Words just won't help. They may listen, but it's as if they can't hear. But deeds will get through. Over the next few months you can demonstrate how it works by staying clean and by getting on with your recovery. They may not believe what you say, but they will believe what they see with their own eyes. Don't play the game 'How Can I Stay Sober If You Don't Trust Me?' As the months pass, their scepticism will disappear and they will be delighted to see you changing before their very eyes.

Partners, wives and husbands

Most partners are overjoyed when their addict or alcoholic stops drinking or using drugs and joins AA or NA. But some, just like the family of the addict, remain suspicious. They have been so hurt that it takes time and the continued recovery of their partner before they can trust again.

Partners also sometimes feel very jealous of AA or NA. For years they have been trying to get their partners off drink and drugs, and it is wounding for them to see another succeeding where they have apparently failed. This is made worse when the addict or alcoholic seems to spend more time at meetings than he or she did drinking or taking drugs.

Of course, if partners go to Al-anon or Families Anonymous they will begin to understand what is happening and that it is the programme of recovery that helps addicts and alcoholics if they accept it. But, once again, you cannot force your partner to attend, any more than he or she could force you to stop taking drugs or drink.

Most upsetting of all to a recovering addict or alcoholic is the relationship which breaks up *after* recovery. Yet the sad truth is that a few people do not like their addict or alcoholic when he or she is well. Consciously or unconsciously, they preferred them sick. It is a fact that a significant percentage of relationships break up *when the alcoholic or addict stops using drink or drugs*. Partners no longer feel needed. They are so damaged that they cannot handle an equal relationship.

Louis, a recovering alcoholic, was married to a social worker. 'She didn't like me as a rolling around 24-hours-a-day drunk, and at first when I sobered up in AA we went through a honeymoon period. It was wonderful.

'Then things started to go wrong. I wouldn't let her manipulate me. I started saying to her: "Don't you think you should consult me about this?" A kind of power battle started up. She wanted to keep the role of family fixer, or be the one who copes with everything.

'I couldn't understand what was happening. She wasn't going to Al-anon, which didn't help our relationship. In her every action it was as if she was telling me "I don't like you sober."

'I remember a dreadful row we had. I went to bed in a different room that night, and at 2 a.m. she woke me up and started a tirade. It was as if she wanted to provoke me, wanted to make me hit her.

'In the end she said to me, "I want you out. I want you out of the house now." So I left. I didn't drink, but I did feel desperate at the time. It was dreadful, but somehow I survived it with the help of AA friends who had been through the same experience.'

Faced with this kind of situation at home, addicts and alcoholics who are newly off drugs and drink need to concentrate on staying clean and sober – and accepting the things they cannot change. It always helps when you find a fellow-member who has been through the same experience. Sharing your pain will heal the wounds faster.

Drugs and drink in others

Sometimes when relationships do not get better it is because there is a problem of drink or drugs in the family or in the partner. When you were using drugs or drinking yourself, you probably did not notice it. Now you are clean and sober, this kind of problem may become evident.

Recovering addicts and alcoholics sometimes think other people are not chemically dependent unless the other's pattern of using drugs or drinking is similar to their own. They are so anxious not to imagine the illness in others that they are often slow to recognise it.

Many addicts come from families where there is a drinking problem or a hidden problem of tranquilliser dependence. If this is the case, other drug users or drinkers may be far from enthusiastic about your recovery. Seeing you clean and sober makes them feel worse about their continued drug-taking or drinking. Because they feel so bad about themselves, they may sneer at NA or AA. They may even try to persuade you that alcohol or the wrongly named 'soft' drugs cannot hurt you.

Alison is somebody who discovered that there was a drink problem in her family. 'My mother probably has a drinking problem. I told her about AA and she was horrified. It was one and a half years after I'd joined, and I tried to talk to her about it. But it was no use.

'She's always tried to make me drink again. When I come to visit her, she'll be at the door saying "Red or white wine, darling?" Or she'll offer pâté and say "Lovely pâté. Lots of brandy in it!" and I'll say "Ma, I really can't eat this." Last time we went to dinner, she produced a pudding and said: "Dig down deep. Lots of lovely alcohol at the bottom." It's the thing I dislike most. I find it so hurtful.'

Some newly recovering addicts, enthusiastic about NA's power to help others recover, go all out to try to 'convert' the family member who is drinking or taking drugs. They are surprised, upset and even resentful when their offers of help are refused.

They have to realise that they cannot force their family into recovery – just as their family could not force them. In the first year of their own recovery it is best for them to concentrate on getting well themselves. Later, when they have some solid months of staying clean and sober behind them, they will probably find that Families Anonymous or Al-anon can help their relationship with the drug user or drinker.

Adult children of alcoholics

You may look back over the years and see that there was alcoholism in the past. Children of alcoholics, even quite young children, are emotionally damaged by the distortions of family life that result from active alcoholism. Many of them took responsibility for their parents, either trying to help the drinking partner or trying to make it up to the unhappy non-drinking partner. This over-developed feeling of responsibility for others persists into other relationships.

The other difficulty that children of alcoholics face is that they do not have any experience of normal, happy relationships. Having lived in a chaotic alcoholic home, they have no idea what a happy home should be like. This may make it difficult for them to choose normal partners in life. Relationships of trust are difficult for the children of chemically dependent parents.

Fortunately, there are sometimes Al-anon groups for the adult children of alcoholics where you may find help to overcome the damage of the past.

Relapses after long-term sobriety

Unfortunately, chemical dependence is a relapsing illness, no matter how long you have been clean and sober. As we have said before, the susceptibility to drugs or drink remains. An addict or an alcoholic is never cured.

Relapses often occur when NA or AA members begin to take sobriety for granted. They stop working at the Twelve Steps and feel that they have their drugs or drink problem beaten for ever. Sometimes they drift away from meetings. At other times they keep up their meetings, but it is merely surface compliance.

Sometimes they simply get bored with NA or AA. Occasional periods of boredom or disenchantment do not matter as long as you keep going to meetings and remember why you are there. One easy cure for boredom is to get involved in helping addicts or alcoholics who are still using drugs or still drinking. It reminds you how lucky you are to be clean and sober.

There is a very quick check you can run on yourself any time that you begin to feel bored or disenchanted with NA or AA. Ask yourself the following questions.

1. *Do I have a home NA or AA group?*
If not, why not? The advantage of regular attendance at the same NA meeting is that people get to know you and you can get close to them. Because they know you, they are likely to notice if your thinking is moving away from the Twelve-Step programme. They will also notice odd behaviour. That way, they may be able to warn you in time if you are drifting towards a relapse.

2. *Am I in regular touch with my sponsor?*
The idea of having a sponsor is that you have somebody who knows all about you to whom you can talk if difficulties arise. It's no good having a sponsor whom you never see or never talk to (though you need not be ringing them ceaselessly). If you haven't got a sponsor, does it mean that you think you can manage without one? Or that you don't want somebody to know all about you?

3. *Am I working on the Twelve Steps?*
You don't have to be a saint, but you should be leading a life which more or less conforms to your and other members' interpretation of the Twelve Steps. If you have decided that you can do without them, then you are risking much unhappiness. Is there something in your life that you are not feeling good about? Resentments, self-pity, guilty secrets or defiant behaviour could all be signs that you are heading for trouble.

4. *What am I doing for the addict or alcoholic who still suffers?*
Helping other addicts and alcoholics is an essential part of recovery, and if you are not doing it, you are taking risks with your own sobriety. You can help others by volunteering for Twelve-Step calls, doing volunteer phone duty, helping run a meeting, helping order literature, taking care of the tea and coffee, or putting out the chairs for a meeting. Practical involvement in NA or AA should be continued, for without it you put your sobriety at grave risk. Not being regularly involved may be the first sign that you are drifting away.

Staying clean and keeping happy

You do not have to have a relapse. Many people have never taken a drink or a mood-altering drug since the first day that they went to an AA or an NA meeting. You will easily find individuals who have enjoyed twenty or thirty years of sober living.

As you get to know these people, you will also discover that they are the doers not the talkers. They have taken the principles of recovery into their daily lives and tried to apply them with determination and humour. The best NA and AA members have the ability to laugh at themselves.

Most people who come into NA or AA have no idea how much happiness awaits them. Recovery isn't fast. Many recovering addicts get impatient and want it all at once, but it takes years rather than months.

But in time most people do feel remarkably happy in their lives. Being in NA or AA does not protect you from the ordinary painful moments and the occasional real tragedies that life brings to all human beings. But most people find that it does give life a new meaning and a new happiness.

You can be one of them.

PART FOUR

For Social Workers, Teachers, Employers and Members of the Helping Professions

11

Diagnosing and Treating Chemical Dependence

As chemical dependence spreads in our society, more and more professional people will come across the problems of addiction and alcoholism. Doctors, magistrates, social workers, solicitors, probation officers, voluntary workers, clergymen, teachers, personnel officers, marriage-guidance counsellors, union officials – all these people have dealings with the social problems caused by drug dependence or alcoholism.

Unfortunately, many of these professions have little if any real knowledge of chemical dependence. Their training ignores the topic altogether, or puts forward out-of-date ideas about it. No wonder they as individuals find themselves baffled, upset or highly irritated when they come to deal with addicts or alcoholics.

Trying to help these people, if they are still using drugs or drinking, is truly a bewildering and maddening experience. Despite genuinely heartfelt promises and occasional periods of progress, their behaviour shows no long-term sign of change. Nor will it, unless the addict or alcoholic comes off drugs and drink altogether.

Many professional workers have had no training in recognising the problem in the first place. They may concentrate all their efforts on helping people with their behavioural or environmental problems, such as health, housing, money or family, without seeing that these stem from drug-using or drinking.

Unfortunately, our society itself refuses to recognise the early stages of drug or drink dependence. The heroin addict with dark glasses, emaciated body and track marks down the arm is recognised as a drug addict; the middle-aged housewife on tranquillisers is not. In the same way, the meths drinker living rough is recognised as an alcoholic, but the middle-class company director whose work is erratic is simply diagnosed as suffering from 'executive stress'.

In particular, society ignores the problems of alcoholism. While newspaper headlines about drugs are common, there is much less concern about drink. Yet for every drug addict there are twenty alcoholics in our society.

Recognising the problem in its early stages

Chemical dependence is a progressive illness, which over the years robs sufferers of their health, their happiness and often their lives. The longer it goes on, the more difficult it is for the sufferer, whether a drug addict or an alcoholic, to recover. In the early stages of chemical dependence, just as in any other illness, recovery is much easier than in the later stages when the addiction has taken such a firm grip.

Yet many professional workers either fail to recognise the illness in its early stages, or for reasons of social embarrassment, wishful thinking, loyalty, or misplaced kindness, do not confront or let the problems confront the addict or the alcoholic. In this way, they rob a sick person of their chance of an early recovery.

Failing to treat the illness in its early stages is not a kindness to the addict or the alcoholic. As we have said, it is like letting a woman with a small cancer lump in her breast go away untreated, leaving it to become a near terminal condition.

The result is that the addicts and alcoholics get more and more damaged and sick. Society is giving them permission to continue on the downward path. They become more and more ill, and more and more desperately unhappy.

Tell-tale signs of addiction or alcoholism

In Chapter 3 we gave some of the tell-tale signs of chemical dependence. For people living in close contact with a drug user or drinker, these signs are helpful. But many professional workers are not in such close contact. They may see the addict or the alcoholic only in the office, rather than in home surroundings. Addicts and alcoholics are past masters at putting on a good front when dealing with authority or people outside the home.

The best way to find out if they have a drug or drink problem is to ask a family member – parents, partners, or sisters and brothers. These usually know enough about the relative's way of life to realise what is going on, though they may be slow to use the word 'alcoholic' or 'addict' because they tend to look only at the meths drinker as alcoholic or the Piccadilly 'fixer' as an addict.

If you are asking a family member, make sure it is someone stable. Addicts and alcoholics sometimes marry or live with people with the same problem. Sometimes a family feels stigmatised by the illness of one of the members and therefore denies the problem.

In addition to asking the family, you may be able to get an idea of the problem from various records. In the later stages of chemical dependence, the addict or alcoholic often becomes ill, has difficulties at work, or difficulties with the law.

Medical signs of chemical dependence

Before drug dependence or alcoholism itself is diagnosed, other diagnoses might precede it. These include stomach ulcers, cirrhosis of the liver, pancreatitis, heart disease, peripheral neuritis, anxiety state, depression, and even impotence. Repeated visits to the doctor for minor aches and pains, of a kind likely to get a painkiller prescription, or repeated 'lost' prescriptions may conceal drug dependence. Addicts have been known to turn up in surgery with a perfectly healthy arm in a sling in order to get a prescription. Frequent broken appointments or inappropriate late-night telephone calls are also a sign of the illness.

Signs of chemical dependence at work

Absence from work on Mondays and days after holidays, absence from work on Friday afternoons, unduly numerous absences for minor illnesses such as 'flu or gastric upset, working during overtime periods (to raise money for drink or drugs), padded expenses, long lunch breaks, lack of concentration or rational thinking after lunch, complaints of 'stress', decrease in job performance, grandiose behaviour, requests for salary advances, financial dishonesty.

Signs of chemical dependence in relationships

Divorce, separation, domestic disputes about money, frequent rows at home, late-night phone calls for no good reason, wife battering, baby battering, promiscuous sexual relationships.

Criminal convictions and chemical dependence

Drunk and disorderly charges, possession of drugs charges, drunk-driving, shoplifting, non-payment of fines, prostitution and importuning charges. Broken appointments with probation services are another possible sign.

It is a cluster of these signs, rather than any single one on its own, that is likely to point to chemical dependence. For instance, not all prostitutes are addicts or alcoholics. However, a person charged with prostitution offences who also has a record of drug possession charges is probably using prostitution as a way of raising money for his or her drug habit.

Similarly, not all people with stomach ulcers are heavy drinkers. However, medical records of ulcers combined with a conviction for drunk-driving points to alcoholism.

Helping the drug-using addict or the drinking alcoholic

Many professionals spend a great deal of their time and energy trying to help addicts or alcoholics in the hope that if their outward circumstances are improved they may do something about their drugs or drinking.

Quite often addicts or alcoholics put up a very good case for that help. They say, and indeed they honestly believe it to be true, that they would be more likely to stop drugs if they were in a new environment. Or they maintain that they only drink because their outward circumstances are so desperate.

'People used to feel sorry for me because I looked thin and I looked ill,' recalls Ricky, whose story is told in Chapter 1. 'When you take drugs, you turn nice. You start talking nice. Most addicts are very nice people and they can manipulate very well. It's only when they haven't got the drug that they can turn nasty.

'I had a probation officer who was very good, but I just manipulated him by not telling the truth, by *not* telling him how much I was taking.'

Alibis and excuses are a way of life for addicts and alcoholics. They are not only conning those around them, they are also desperately conning themselves. The truth is that helping them with their outward circumstances *before* they stop using drugs or drinking is a waste of energy. Changing the environment does not change the person if that person is chemically dependent.

We did not believe this when we first came into contact with addicts, even though we were told it. 'In particular,' writes Jim Ditzler, 'I wasted a lot of time and energy when I was working in a vocational rehabilitation centre in the USA. I was put in charge of career problems.

'My superior in the office told me that it was no use helping addicts and alcoholics *until* they had stopped using drugs and stopped drinking. It was just a waste of my time. The time to help them was when they had been off the drugs and drink for some time.

'I did not believe him. The alcoholics came to me and told me "What I need is a job. Then I will be able to get my drinking under control." I would go to enormous lengths to help them, giving them tests, looking round for opportunities, and then at the last minute they wouldn't show up.

'I began to see that I was a complete fool who was just being sucked in by their hard-luck stories. I began to approach the problem in the opposite order. First I would find them treatment for their alcohol and addiction problems, and then help them find a job after they came out of treatment. In that order, it worked.'

Treating underlying psychological problems

The other great waste of time and energy is to treat addicts and alcoholics for their underlying psychological problems while they are still using drugs or drinking. It is like trying to play chess with somebody when they are under an anaesthetic.

True, addicts and alcoholics display quite remarkable emotional and behavioural disorders, but many of these are the result of, not the cause of, their drug-using or drinking. If drugs or drink are stopped, many of these problems fall away.

'I went to see lots of psychiatrists while I was using heroin,' remembers Carol, a twenty-nine-year-old addict who is three years into recovery. 'It didn't work. They would usually tell me to stop taking heroin and put me on tranquillisers. I was also put in a lot of nursing homes, but there was no follow-up treatment afterwards. I just went out and started using again. I didn't know what else to do.

'Once I was put in a behaviour-modification centre. It was all done on rewards and punishments. I had to learn how to behave and be good. I left that place and after two months I went back on heroin.'

Addicts and alcoholics sometimes do need therapy for their emotional disorders, but they need it *after* they have stopped using drugs and drink. That is the time that some of them need professional help, in order to learn how to live a new and happy life.

Treating addicts with drugs

Giving addicts prescribed drugs to get them off illegal drugs is not only a waste of resources; we believe it also delays their eventual recovery. Methadone maintenance treatment usually just makes heroin addicts into methadone addicts. Likewise, giving an alcoholic tranquillisers simply turns an alcoholic into a tranquilliser addict. It is like giving brown sugar, instead of white, to a diabetic!

Of course, many addicts and alcoholics beg for substitute drugs, because they see it as the easy way out. They cannot envisage life without some kind of chemical crutch. Unfortunately, the prescribed drugs, whether methadone, benzodiazepines, Temgesic (buprenorphine) or DF 118 (dihydrocodeine tartrate) are all highly addictive for addicts and alcoholics. They abuse these drugs for their mood-altering effects.

Tranquillisers in particular have more prolonged withdrawals than either alcohol or illegal drugs, so that keeping addicts on prescribed drugs lands them in even greater difficulty when they want to come off.

Besides, addicts are rarely truthful about their drug habit. 'When I got put on a methadone programme, it was meant to be a reducing programme,' recalls Carol. 'But I never got it reduced. Every time I went to the clinic they'd say "How about a lower methadone script?" I would make up excuses why not. I'd say "If you lower my methadone I'll go out and use heroin." The irony of this was that I *was* scoring heroin anyway, even though I was on the methadone programme. Especially at weekends. I'd score then, as I didn't count weekends.'

Indeed, methadone is widely available on the black market, because many addicts collect their methadone prescriptions, sell the methadone and buy heroin with the proceeds! Others simply add heroin and other illegal drugs on top of the methadone they are taking, sometimes with fatal results.

There is a further problem facing drug-dependence clinics. Each clinic spawns a network of patients who know each other and swap information about drugs – where to get them, what quality is available, current prices of methadone on the black market as well as current illegal drug prices, which doctors can be conned for a prescription and what is the best story to tell to them. Doctors who are generous with their prescribing often find themselves with a host of new clients.

Drugs lead back to the drug of choice

Addicts who have stayed off drugs for a time often recall how taking prescribed drugs eventually led them back to their drug of choice. Heroin addicts who stay off heroin for a time, either on methadone, tranquillisers or alcohol, often end up back on heroin itself.

'I did manage to give up heroin for a few days,' remembers Susan. 'But whenever I did this I always substituted with another drug. I wouldn't leave the house without a bag of tranquillisers. I was also drinking very heavily and smoking dope.

'My fiancé used drugs too. With him I managed to scrape together enough money to get treatment from a private doctor. We were paying the doctor to give us substitute drugs to make it easier to get off heroin. At the same time we were still taking the heroin. It sounds completely insane, but it illustrates how I couldn't control the habit.'

Each time Susan went off heroin, she turned to tranquillisers or alcohol as a substitute. Each time, she went back to heroin eventually. A year and a half later she found Narcotics Anonymous, has stayed off all drugs for nearly two years since and is enjoying life.

'I don't have to use drugs, any drugs at all, or drink now. I am truly grateful for that each day. But I am sure I wouldn't be clean now except for NA. I know from the amount of times I tried to stop using, that I couldn't do it on my own.'

Sometimes addicts or alcoholics simply make a complete switch. They discover that the new drug, whatever it is, is just as good as their old one. Ricky, who became first a heroin addict and then (when he had given up heroin) an alcoholic, is a good example of this. His story in Chapter 1 shows what a devastating effect alcohol had on him. Because of the progressive deterioration of his illness, alcohol brought him down to sleeping rough – something that had not happened to him while he was on heroin.

Nor do drugs work any better with alcoholics. Giving alcoholics drugs will not stop them using alcohol. Many alcoholics simply take their doctors' prescriptions and drink on top of the pills.

Even those who do not mix pills and booze are not stopped from drinking by taking pills. 'I went to my practitioner and told him I was an alcoholic several years before I went to AA,' says George, a thirty-two-year-old printer, married with two small children. 'He gave me some Hemineverin and I stopped drinking. Religiously I took those pills and I didn't have a drink. My wife watched me like a hawk. And when they were finished, I went and had a drink. A bottle of whisky in twelve hours.'

Nor is Antabuse (disulfiram) or Abstem (citrated calcium carbimide) a long-term answer. Alcoholics will simply stop taking the Antabuse tablets and start drinking again. Even knowing the dangers, some alcoholics simply drink on top of these pills and get violently sick.

Neither drug dependence nor alcoholism can be medicated away.

Abstinence is the only answer

The addict or the alcoholic must be forcefully told that abstinence from all mood-altering chemicals is the only answer. To suggest that there are easier ways of getting well is to delay the final recovery.

Many professional people try to offer easier solutions – not least because addicts and alcoholics often refuse point blank to do without any drugs at all. We all want to be liked by others – even by our clients. There is therefore a strong temptation not to confront addicts and alcoholics with the unpleasant truth. It's not cricket to be too explicit – except about cricket!

As a result, an alcoholic may be told to try to cut down his drinking rather than to cease altogether – something that he cannot in the long term achieve. Many professional people who are social drinkers themselves simply cannot grasp the idea that an alcoholic cannot drink moderately in the long term. Or they advise the alcoholic to cut down or go without alcohol for only a certain amount of time, with the promise that he can drink again. All this does is make the alcoholic fit enough to drink again – and it is just what any alcoholic wants to hear, though deep down he knows it's a lie.

Fortunately, heroin addicts are not told they can use their drug in moderation. It is far more likely that they may be told that cannabis, tranquillisers or alcohol cannot harm them as much – advice that is based simply on ignorance or on the adviser's wishful thinking.

Quite often, when alcoholics or addicts are faced by the hard truth, they react with anger and self-pity. This is part of the inner denial that is characteristic of almost all alcoholics and addicts. It takes personal courage to tell them that their drug or drink habit will only get worse unless they stop all mood-altering drugs. It also takes courage to refuse to help unless they do something serious about their drinking or drug-using. Yet refusing to help is the kindest thing to do. In the long term it is no help just to 'paint over the rust'.

When an addict or an alcoholic is willing to stop drugs or drink, it is important strongly to recommend frequent attendance at NA or AA meetings. A lukewarm suggestion will be ineffective. Research has shown that when the therapist warmly and firmly recommends these organisations, the addict or alcoholic is much more likely to follow the recommendation. Remember, addicts and alcoholics need help not just to stop but to stay stopped for ever.

Alcoholics Anonymous and Narcotics Anonymous are not just for 'last-hope' cases. Nor are they solely for middle-class clients. These myths abound because a staggering number of those who deal with alcoholics and addicts have never gone to an AA or NA meeting.

We believe that those who treat addicts and alcoholics for their problem should go to at least twenty AA or NA meetings. Anything less than this means that they miss the best opportunity of learning how to help others.

You *must* familiarise yourself properly with what these two organisations are doing, how they work, and the kind of people you meet in them. Both NA and AA have open meetings to which outsiders are welcome. All you need to do is ring the phone numbers in Appendix 2 and get the details. It is unprofessional to let personal embarrassment or shyness get in the way of doing this.

By doing it, you can also build up a network of NA or AA contacts in your local area, which can help you a great deal when dealing with clients.

Those who have only occasional dealings with addicts or alcoholics should also go to a number of NA or AA meetings. When they have done this, they are in a much better position to give help. Most professionals who go to these meetings find them absolutely fascinating!

Prison, the law and addiction

At the moment, many addicts and alcoholics come up in the

courts on a variety of charges. Many of them commit acts which rightly earn them prison sentences. Yet the law has no way of helping them do anything about their drug-using or drinking.

Some states in the USA have arrangements whereby drunken drivers have to attend a course on alcohol and alcoholism. They learn about drinking and about the symptoms of alcoholism. Those among them who have a drink problem are encouraged to get help. Judges can also sentence an offender to a compulsory course of, say, thirty Alcoholics Anonymous meetings or to a specific course of rehabilitation in a treatment centre, as an alternative to a fine or prison.

None of these sentencing alternatives exists in Britain. Magistrates can and often do recommend Alcoholics Anonymous or Narcotics Anonymous from the bench, but it remains their personal suggestion.

Nearly all prisons in Britain have regular meetings of Alcoholics Anonymous, and Narcotics Anonymous are just beginning to hold their meetings in prison too. If you are a probation officer, prison visitor or magistrate, it is imperative to suggest these meetings to the offender.

We believe it would be money well spent to set up programmes for addicts and alcoholics within the prison system. As it is, too many of these ill people receive no help at all, and come out of prison only to go back on drugs and drink. Soon they commit more crimes to support their habit. Society is the loser when their illness goes untreated.

Letting the addict face the consequences

It is no favour to the addict or alcoholic, however, to let him escape the consequences of his drug-using or drinking. Prison sentences are rightly given to those who commit serious crimes, no matter what their reasons. Indeed, prison sentences can be helpful, as Ricky's story in Chapter 1 shows.

'Prison did me a lot of good,' says more than one recovering addict. 'I was in such a state when I went in there that it probably saved my life. It gave me time to think. I've been clean in Narcotics Anonymous since coming out.'

Just as the family should stand back and let the addict suffer the consequences of his drug-using, so should others. Rescuing addicts or alcoholics from the consequences of their behaviour simply delays their recovery.

This is hard for the 'helping' professional to grasp. Their training has usually been to suggest that helping people will give

Millionaire's ex-wife on drugs charge goes free

Kitty Bentley

KITTY BENTLEY, heroin addict daughter of the Marchioness of Bute, escaped jail on a drugs charge yesterday after a magistrate was told of her fight to kick the killer habit.

Instead the 29-year-old ex-wife of millionaire businessman John Bentley was ordered into a court's cells for four hours and then freed.

She admitted having 190 milligrams of heroin in Kensington High Street and being in breach of a two-year probation order imposed for a similar offence at Knightsbridge Crown Court a year earlier.

Mr Eric Crowther the-Horseferry Road magistrate, asked her if she felt she could beat her addiction. Mrs Bentley replied: "I am doing my best."

"Why somebody like you should do this is a mystery," the magistrate told her. "Basically, you are a young lady from a wealthy background, just the sort of lady who the leeches who sell drugs like to batten to."

Miss Sheena Bayne, defending, had urged the magistrates to free Mrs Bentley so that she could be treated in America. She was booked into a clinic in Minnesota for a two months' course followed by ten months in a halfway house there.

"She is absolutely desperate to kick this habit and to sort her life out" said Miss Bayne.

Mrs Bentley gave an address in Cottesmore Gardens, Kensington, but Miss Bayne said that to get away from the London drugs scene she had been living with her parents in Scotland since her arrest.

Mr Barry Press, prosecuting, told the court that Mrs Bentley was arrested with the heroin after leaving a hotel which police were watching.

BIRTHDAY HONOURS LIST

Mrs Lynda Chalker
(PC)

Miss Joan Hickson
(OBE)

Grp. Capt. Hugh Dundas
(Knight)

Chesterton, OBE, Architect and
Town Planner.

Miss Elizabeth Viole
Maconchy, CBE (Mrs Le Fanu)
Composer.

KBE

David Wigley Nickson, CBE
DL, President, Confederation of

them a better chance of tackling their problems. The reverse is true with drug dependence and alcoholism. 'Helping' or protecting alcoholics or addicts simply enables them to go on drinking or using drugs.

Helping the family of the addict or alcoholic

Where help can be given is to the family members who surround the addict or alcoholic. These are often suffering severely – financially, sometimes physically if they are being abused, always emotionally.

Children, in particular, are at risk in an alcoholic or drug-using home. It is not that their parents do not love them. It is simply that the chaos surrounding the alcoholic or addict affects their lives too. Their lives are, above all, emotionally chaotic. The alcoholic or addicted parent is one moment kind and caring, the next an angry, raving stranger. There is no emotional security in their lives. Physical and sometimes sexual abuse is quite common too. Fear is their constant companion.

It is important that children should be told about alcoholism and drug dependence. That way, they have some idea of why these things are happening in their home. Without this knowledge, many children believe that in some way they are to blame, and many make pathetic and frantic efforts to put things right. If they are told about the illness of chemical dependence, this will relieve them of the burden of misplaced responsibility and release them from some of their acute feelings of fear, guilt and sometimes anger.

The fellowships of Al-anon and Families Anonymous are quite crucial here. They can do a great deal to help the suffering families, whether or not the alcoholic or addict stops drinking or using drugs. Once again, a surprising number of helping professionals have never been to their meetings, and are in almost total ignorance of what they do and how they do it. Without seeing for themselves, they may – in the words of one marriage-guidance counsellor who had never bothered to investigate for himself – believe these are just 'tea and coffee sessions'.

Both Al-anon and Families Anonymous offer specific suggestions which can give enormous help to the suffering families, who often bear the brunt of bad behaviour from the alcoholic or addict. There is also an organisation called Alateen for teenage children of alcoholics. Some Al-anon meetings, known as ACA meetings, are for the adult children of alcoholics, to help them deal with the legacy of their disturbed childhoods.

All these organisations are listed in Appendix 2. Just ring and ask for the address of the nearest open meeting.

Teachers and schools can play their part in educating people about drink and drugs. All the self-help groups we have mentioned will provide speakers who will help you understand the problem. Most children find this a great deal more interesting than lectures on the topic.

There is also literature available from the head offices of these organisations. Older teenagers should be encouraged to find out for themselves by going to an open meeting, as part of a school project. Literature, video films and speakers for conferences can also be provided.

Finally, schools need to remember that drug-taking and drinking start at a very young age nowadays. There are children as young as fourteen who are full members of Narcotics Anonymous and Alcoholics Anonymous, whose drug-taking and drinking histories are appalling. Some of them started on drink or drugs as early as ten, eleven or twelve years old.

So some of the children attending our schools already have quite severe drug or alcohol problems. Like all addicts and alcoholics, they need help at the early stages, not at the later stages of the illness. And like all addicts and alcoholics, abstinence is the answer. The sooner this message reaches them, the better their chances of recovery.

Our treatment programme

What we have done is successfully to integrate the caring philosophy of Alcoholics Anonymous into the professional treatment programme. This is a team concept, including counselling, nursing, medical, psychological and psychiatric staff who have had special training and experience with addictive diseases.

In doing this, something profound seems to have occurred – a humanising of a complex treatment programme with the close sharing found in both AA and NA.

Perhaps the most important factor in the programme is the opportunity the patient has to learn and grow in small structured peer groups. There is an immediate effectiveness in the sharing of a common experience. This common identity appears to be based on the admission and acceptance of human limitation. Non-addictive people seem to have no problem in accepting their own limitations. Most addictive people find this reality unacceptable.

In the commonality of accepting limitation, patients draw strength and help from other patients, and in turn help other alcoholic and chemically dependent people to recover. In simple terms, people who have made a career of abusing alcohol or drugs, and who have been dishonest, manipulative and intolerant towards their family and friends, learn to change when confronted with each other and their common, chronic addiction.

In Dr Ernest Kurtz's book on the history of AA, *Not God*, is a fine description of the experience of finding this common identity. He writes of 'the shared honesty of mutual vulnerability openly acknowledged'. This suggests that if one can give up trying to be grandiose or omnipotent as a cover for fear and guilt, and admit one's limitations, then this admission provides the dynamic which makes recovery possible. From this acceptance of limitation, one can rejoin the human race and find a common mutual humanity.

From this human 'peak' or spiritual experience, for the alcoholic or addict comes the courage to face up to the illness of chemical dependence and to recover.

The primary function of any chemical-dependence programme is to evaluate and initiate the proper treatment for people who are suffering from alcohol or drug dependence. We see this illness as dependence on or abuse of alcohol and/or drugs. These drugs can be prescribed or illegal; most patients substitute one for another during their career of dependence.

A wide range of services is provided by the treatment team. We think very few, if any, professionals can work successfully outside a team. It is just too draining and too emotionally stressful.

Based on the patient's history, current physical and emotional condition, employment and family situation, a referral may be made to the out-patients' department at our London centre or at Farm Place, our treatment centre in Ockley, Surrey, or to in-patient treatment at Farm Place. We insist on involvement in the appropriate self-help group of AA or NA.

Out-patient treatment begins with a medical assessment and detoxification, followed by necessary therapy by counselling, group therapy and family counselling – as indicated by the individual treatment plan which is developed by the treatment team.

The patient requiring in-patient treatment receives a full medical examination and is placed on a detoxification regimen if necessary. In order to assist the newly admitted patient to understand the programme, there is an introductory and orientation session explaining the structure of the programme and the patient's responsibilities and rights while in treatment.

Soon after admission, each patient is assessed several times so that an individual treatment plan can be developed. Treatment-plan designs are based on a series of interviews supplemented by co-operation from the family, GP and other referrants – employers and other significant people in the patient's life.

This plan is designed to enable each individual to progress according to his or her capabilities. All patients have frequent sessions of individual counselling to enable them to recognise their dependence on alcohol or drugs and to resolve problems relating to the special needs of each individual and the family members.

Structured group therapy takes place twice daily. By sharing their experiences, patients come to terms with their dependence and the damage this has caused to themselves and to others. With the support of their peers, patients face their mutual problems with chemicals and begin to change.

Families are encouraged to involve themselves in the treatment programme. They participate in multiple family groups and in individual family-counselling sessions. This is to ensure that the family members, or significant others, understand the nature of chemical dependence. This understanding benefits both the patient and the family. Individual treatment plans are developed by the team for families, or significant others, to maximise their involvement. This is sometimes described as a 'family-systems' approach to addiction.

In recent years it has been recognised how much the families of chemically dependent people have become emotionally involved and damaged by association with the illness. The patient has often blamed his need for alcohol and drugs on other people or problems. Usually most families have initially believed this to be the case. They have taken the blame on themselves and have sometimes become immobilised and/or complicit in the illness.

Family programmes must therefore be geared to teach the family to modify their reactive behaviour and to detach from the patient while still caring. Another object is to help the family to know what to expect when the patient comes home. They must learn to live for themselves and not to be a weathervane for the chemically dependent person: to accept that their own personal growth is good for them, and that what is good for them is good for the chemically dependent person.

Of further assistance to the patient are the self-help groups of AA and NA, in which they participate while in treatment and which are their on-going support system in recovery. This applies equally to family members in Al-anon, Alateen and FA.

Early in treatment, each patient is given a psychological assessment, which is communicated directly to them in an understandable way. This is to help the patient to develop increased insight and understanding into the psychological problems that usually develop as addiction progresses and how these problems usually recede as recovery stabilises.

Patients are also assessed to ensure that no serious psychiatric problems, related to chemical dependence or independent of it, are present. This assessment is integrated into the individual treatment plan and updated as appropriate.

Further information is given to patients during treatment in the form of lectures giving guidelines for recovery, ways of coping and the way roles in the family change in recovery.

Exercise and relaxation sessions are provided to enhance the patient's physical and emotional well-being, and also to promote social interaction. Having fun without chemicals is often a new experience which must be learned or relearned after years during which alcohol or drugs have been the main social lubricant.

Some patients need a longer period of treatment than four to six weeks of primary care. Extended care is provided within the residential centre of Farm Place. The aim is to help patients make changes in lifestyle and attitudes, and to develop self-worth without the risk of returning to alcohol and drugs.

Some patients need to spend between six months and a year in a halfway house – usually those who need to be able to spend a long period in a structured environment in which they can take time to consolidate recovery. This is necessary for some young people with a long drug history and little structure in their life, and for alcoholics with a previous extensive history of relapse. The halfway house provides counselling and on-going group therapy, as well as opportunities to work, continue education and progress to normal living while involvement in AA or NA is developing.

Plans are made to ensure, as far as possible, that the patient has the best chance for recovery. After-care services include introduction to the appropriate self-help group, out-patient follow-up and group therapy. The main goal of after-care is to continue progress made in treatment and to work towards happiness and normal living. All patients are followed for at least five years.

Recovery really begins when the patient returns home to use the tools that have been given and the skills acquired with the on-going assistance of the self-help groups of AA and NA.

Our success rate

Those who specialise in the treatment of alcoholism or drug dependence know that it is not easy to treat alcoholics and addicts together. We do.

The most important British study of the decade, at an eminent London hospital, followed up one hundred alcoholics from stable family and work backgrounds at six, twelve, eighteen and twenty-four months after hospital in-patient treatment. It showed that by the two-year mark there was a 100-per-cent relapse rate: all the patients so treated had gone back to drinking over this period. A recent important ten-year follow-up at a number of London drug clinics showed that 53 per cent of addicts had either died or continued to be maintained on drugs. Only 38 per cent were abstinent from illegal drugs.

Our treatment results are much better. Our follow-up studies over five years include all patients, even those who did not fully complete treatment with us. Patients in the study ranged from very disturbed young addicts to alcoholics in their sixties. All patients were followed up at six-month intervals for five years after treatment.

Conservatively, fifty out of every hundred patients were totally abstinent. A further twenty-five had had a relapse, usually of short length after leaving the clinic, but had gone back to abstinence, successfully continued in recovery and improved the quality of their lives.

These short-term relapsers were often the young and impulsive addicts or alcoholics. Though persuaded that they had a drink and/or drug problem, nevertheless they made one final effort to prove the treatment wrong. Their relapse instead acted as a final convincer that abstinence from all mood-altering chemicals was the only answer.

A final twenty-five addicts and alcoholics relapsed after treatment and had to be re-hospitalised or required further long-term treatment. Among these were many who had left treatment early.

These results show that treating alcoholics and addicts is not a waste of time or money, and that, with the right treatment, a high degree of success can be expected. Some patients, indeed, have an even better prognosis. Referrals from employers or unions with a policy of treatment and support for alcoholism and drug dependence, instead of dismissal or covering up the problem, can expect a 75–80-per-cent recovery rate without any relapse.

*   *   *

Treating alcoholics and addicts has great rewards. We see them arrive for treatment as sick, miserable people, leading destructive lives; but as their recovery progresses they become happy, stable, achieving people, full of life.

Change is the key that turns misery into a walking miracle.

APPENDIX 1

Tranquillisers and Sleeping Pills

If you are taking tranquillisers or sleeping pills, you should first of all check exactly what the drug is. Most tranquillisers and sleeping pills belong to the benzodiazepine family. Tranquillisers and sleeping pills are interchangeable, so if you don't find your sleeping pill in the list below, check under tranquillisers. Likewise, if your tranquilliser is not under the tranquilliser heading, you may find it listed under sleeping pills. Here are the drugs in alphabetical order, with their brand names and dosages. Your pills may be prescribed under their scientific name or under a brand name.

Benzodiazepine sleeping pills

An asterisk denotes a long-acting drug.

Scientific name	Brand names	Low dose	High dose	Very high dose
Flunitrazepam* Tablets: 1mg	Rohypnol	0.5–1mg	1.5–2mg	over 2mg
Flurazepam* Capsules: 15mg and 30mg	Dalmane Paxane	15mg	30mg	over 30mg
Loprazolam Tablets: 1mg	Dormonoct	1mg	1.5–2mg	over 2mg

Scientific name	Brand names	Low dose	High dose	Very high dose
Lormetazepam Capsules: 1mg Tablets: 500 microgms and 1mg	Loromet Noctamid	0.5mg	1mg	over 1mg
Nitrazepam* Capsules: 5mg Tablets: 5mg and 10mg Elixir: 2.5mg per 5ml	Mogadon Nitrados Noctesed Remnos Somnite Surem Unisomnia	5mg	10mg	over 10mg
Temazepam Capsules: 10mg, 15mg, 20mg and 30mg Elixir: 10mg per 5ml	Euhypnos Euhypnos 10 Euhypnos 20 Normison	10–20mg	30–60mg	over 60mg
Triazolam Tablets: 125 and 250 microgms	Halcion	125 microgms	250 microgms	over 250 microgms

Benzodiazepine tranquillisers

Because tranquillisers are often taken more than once a day, the dosages given here are the total for one day. An asterisk denotes a long-acting drug.

Scientific name	Brand names	Low dose	High dose	Very high dose
Alprazolam Tablets: 250 and 500 microgms	Xanax	500–1250 microgms	1500–3000 microgms	over 3000 microgms
Bromazepam* Tablets: 1.5mg and 3mg	Lexotan	3–9mg	10.5–18mg	over 18mg
Chlor-diazepoxide* Capsules: 5mg and 10mg Tablets: 5mg, 10mg and 25mg	Librium Tropium	10–35mg	40–100mg	over 100mg
Clobazam* Capsules: 10mg	Frisium	10–20mg	30–40mg	over 40mg

Scientific name	Brand names	Low dose	High dose	Very high dose
Clorazepate dipotassium* Capsules: 7.5mg and 15mg	Tranxene	7.5mg	15mg	22.5mg and over
Diazepam* Capsules: 2mg, 5mg and 10mg Tablets: 2mg, 5mg and 10mg Elixir: 2mg per 5ml Suppositories: 5mg and 10mg	Valium Alupram Atensine Diazemuls Evacalm Solis Stesolid Tensium Valrelease	2–10mg	12–30mg	over 30mg
Ketazolam* Capsules: 15mg and 30mg	Anxon	15–30mg	45–60mg	over 60mg
Lorazepam Tablets: 1mg and 2.5mg	Almazine Ativan	1–2mg	2.5–5mg	over 5mg
Medazepam* Capsules: 5mg and 10mg	Nobrium	10–15mg	20–30mg	over 30mg
Oxazepam Tablets: 10mg, 15mg and 30mg Capsules: 30mg	Oxanid Serenid-D Serenid Forte	30–45mg	60–120mg	over 120mg
Prazepam* Tablets: 10mg	Centrax	10–20mg	30–40mg	over 40mg

The dosages in the above chart have been calculated to give you some idea of how heavy a dose you are taking. Some drugs are taken several times a day, so the chart gives a total dose over a 24-hour period.

Do not be deceived by the fact that you are on a low dose. Even low doses taken for months can have painful withdrawal effects. The drugs come in the form of tablets, capsules and occasionally in liquid elixirs which vary in strength. So to calculate the dose you are taking, you will need to know the strength of each tablet then to multiply by the number of tablets you are taking.

If you are taking a sleeping pill or tranquilliser that is neither in this chart nor is a new drug, you may be taking a barbiturate or similar drug. A list of barbiturate drugs appears later in this appendix. People coming off barbiturates or similar drugs *must* do so under medical supervision – so ask your doctor for help.

How to come off tranquillisers and sleeping pills

These instructions apply only to the benzodiazepine drugs listed above. The reason why dosages are listed is because you need to come off a high dose more slowly than off a low dose. Remember to add in *all* the benzodiazepine drugs you are taking, both sleeping pills and daytime tranquillisers. For instance, if you are taking a low dose of tranquillisers and a low dose of sleeping pills, added together these put you in the high-dose category. Coming off tranquillisers or sleeping pills too fast is dangerous. Do not stop your pills abruptly. The proper way to come off these drugs is to take smaller and smaller doses, taking them at the same time intervals. It is *not* safe simply to leave longer times between taking the drugs.

It is always best to withdraw from tranquillisers with the supervision of a doctor. But if this is not possible, you can follow the instructions below, which are based on a withdrawal plan worked out by Professor Malcolm Lader of the Institute of Psychiatry. This is a minimum-time withdrawal: *you must not withdraw any faster*.

If you are taking a low dose

You must take at least a month tapering off the drug. To do this, you should divide your daily dose by five and reduce it by a fifth each week.

If you are taking a high dose

You must take at least six weeks tapering off the drug. To do this, divide by seven and reduce it by a seventh each week. As the mathematics of this may not be easy, you could take an extra week and divide by 8 if this will make it more simple.

If you are taking a very high dose

You must have medical supervision to withdraw. Ask your doctor for help. If he does not help you, then take advice from NA members about finding a new doctor or a drug-dependence clinic that will help. If you are withdrawing from these pills as an outpatient, then the dose should be reduced over eight weeks or more. Remember, reducing too fast is not safe.

Reducing the dose

In order to reduce your tranquilliser dose correctly, it will be helpful to ask your doctor to prescribe tablets of a lower strength, say 2mg diazepam tablets rather than 5mg. If this is not possible, then break the tablets into halves and quarters.

The mathematics of reducing the dose are not always easy. With long-acting tranquillisers (asterisked in the chart above) which are being taken three times a day, you can reduce the midday dose by a little bit more than the others if this will help the mathematics. For example, if you are on 30mg of Valium (diazepam) daily, you need to reduce the dose over six weeks. The following schedule shows how you can do it easily using 5mg and 2mg tablets. It avoids having to fiddle around breaking tablets into tiny fragments.

Week	Morning	Midday	Evening
1	10mg	5mg	10mg
2	5mg	5mg	10mg
3	5mg	5mg	5mg
4	2mg	2mg	5mg
5	2mg	2mg	2mg
6	2mg	—	2mg
7	—	—	2mg

With the other short-acting drugs (those not asterisked in the chart) you must reduce *each* dose by the *same* amount. Some people use a nail-file to file down the tablet to the right size. If you are being given drugs which come in capsules, ask your doctor to prescribe the same drug in tablet form. If, however, the drug does not come in tablet form, ask him to prescribe a similar drug in tablets. Trying to cut down the dose in capsules is just too difficult. You need tablets.

If on reading them you find these instructions difficult to understand, try taking this book to an NA or AA meeting and getting somebody to help you work out your particular withdrawal schedule. It is always best to get a doctor's supervision, if you can. The important thing to remember is this: do not stop these drugs abruptly, but taper off over several weeks. Stopping abruptly is dangerous.

Barbiturate sedatives and sleeping pills

Coming off barbiturates should be done under medical supervision. It is extremely dangerous to stop taking barbiturates abruptly. To help you identify what drugs you are taking, here is a list of barbiturates and brand names.

Barbiturates

Scientific name	Brand name
Amylobarbitone	Amytal
Amylobarbitone sodium	Sodium amytal
Amylobarbitone sodium mixed with quinalbarbitone sodium	Tuinal
Butobarbitone	Soneryl
Cyclobarbitone calcium	Phanodorm
Pentobarbitone sodium	Nembutal
Phenobarbitone	Luminal Phenobarbitone spansule
Quinalbarbitone sodium	Seconal sodium

Other drugs sometimes prescribed as sedatives or sleeping pills

There are also some other drugs which are still occasionally prescribed as sedatives or sleeping pills. If you are taking these, you should get medical advice about how to come off them. It could be dangerous – in some cases very dangerous – to stop taking them abruptly.

Scientific name	Brand name
Chloral hydrate	Chloral mixture Noctec
Chlormethiazole edisylate	Heminevrin
Chlormezanone	Trancopal
Dichloralphenazone	Welldorm
Hydroxyzine hydrochloride	Atarax
Meprobamate	Equanil Meprate Tenavoid
Methyprylone	Noludar
Promethazine hydrochloride	
Triclofos sodium	Triclofos Elixir
Trimeprazine tartrate	

If you are being prescribed sleeping pills, tranquillisers or sedatives which you cannot identify from these lists, you should check back with the doctor giving the prescription before ceasing to take them.

This list of drugs was correct at the end of 1985. New drugs, especially among the benzodiazepine tranquillisers and sleeping pills, may come on the market after this date. In Britain, the current list of drugs available to doctors can be found in the British National Formulary, published yearly by the British Medical Association and the Pharmaceutical Society of Great Britain. Your local library can order a copy for you, though it will take a few weeks to arrive.

Note to readers in Australia, Canada, New Zealand and South Africa

Drugs are sold under different brand names and in different strength tablets and capsules, according to the country in which you live. Drugs which are not sold in the UK may be sold elsewhere, and vice versa. The benzodiazepine sleeping pills and tranquillisers are sold under an amazing number of different brand names in each country. The ones listed in this appendix will not include all the brand names used in your own country.

For proper information about your own drug brand names, consult the Mims guide to prescription drugs which is published in Australia, New Zealand and South Africa. There are also reference books which give Canadian brand names.

APPENDIX 2

Self-Help Groups and Agencies Dealing with Chemical Dependence

These addresses and telephone numbers were collected at the beginning of 1986. By the time you are reading this book, some of them may have changed. If so, simply look in the phone book for the new number.

Great Britain

Narcotics Anonymous, PO Box 246, London SW10. Tel: 01–351 6794. NA is for anybody who wants to stop using drugs – no matter who they are or what drug they are using, including legally prescribed drugs like tranquillisers and sleeping pills.

Alcoholics Anonymous, PO Box 514, 11 Redcliffe Gardens, London SW10 9BG. Tel: 01–352 9779 (Greater London area office 01–834 8202). AA is for anybody who wants to stop drinking. There are local offices in many areas, so consult you local phone book.

Families Anonymous, 88 Caledonian Road, London N1 9DN. Tel: 01–278 8805. FA is for anybody with a relative or friend who is using drugs, including prescribed drugs and glue sniffing. FA will help those who are not yet sure if the problem is one of drugs.

Al-anon Family Groups, 61 Great Dover Street, London SE1 4YF. Tel: 01–403 0888. Al-anon is for anybody who has a relative or friend with a drinking problem. It can help those adults who grew up in an alcoholic home. Alateen, its branch for teenagers, helps young people whose parents or relatives have a drinking problem. Local phone books may have a number. AA offices usually will pass this on, if it is not in the book.

Other agencies

Standing Conference on Drug Abuse, 1–4 Hatton Place, Hatton Garden, London EC1N 8ND. Tel: 01–430 2341. SCODA can supply a list of hospitals which provide a service for drug users, a list of residential rehabilitation places for drug users, and a list of advisory services and day projects for drug users. Send a large stamped addressed envelope for these.

Republic of Ireland

Narcotics Anonymous, PO Box 1368, Sherriff Street, Dublin 1. No Dublin phone number was available in 1985. Phone London NA office on 01–351 6794 for details of local meetings.

Alcoholics Anonymous, 26 Essex Quay, Dublin 8. Tel: Dublin 774809 or 714050.

Families Anonymous, 88 Caledonian Road, London N1 9DN. Tel: 01–278 8805 for details of meetings in Eire. In 1985 there were FA meetings in Dublin, though the central office was in London.

Al-anon, 61 Great Dover Street, London SE1 4YF. Tel: 01–403 0888. The London office deals with enquiries about meetings in Eire.

Australia

Narcotics Anonymous, PO Box 440, Leichandt, New South Wales 2040. Tel: 02–810 2020. There are also other NA offices in other major cities, so check your phone directory to see if there is one near you.

Alcoholics Anonymous, PO Box 5321, Sydney, New South Wales 2001. Tel: 02–290 2210. Also many local AA offices.

Families Anonymous. There is no general office, but in 1985 there was an FA meeting being held in Melbourne. Up-to-date information from Families Anonymous, PO Box 528, Van Nuys, California 91408.

Nar Anon, PO Box Q108, Queen Victoria Building, Sydney, New South Wales 2000. Tel: 02–300 9736. Nar-Anon is another organisation for the families of those addicted to drugs.

Al-anon Family Groups, PO Box 1002H, Melbourne, Victoria 3001. Tel: 03–62 4933.

Other agencies

In so far as there is a national organisation, it is the **Alcohol and Drug Foundation**, PO Box 477, Canberra City, ACT 2601. There are plans for an emergency phone service in all capital cities in the future with a national (008) number.

In addition there are the following state organisations:

New South Wales
Alcohol and Drug Information Service, St Vincent's Hospital, Sydney. Tel: 02–331 2111. 24-hour service of advice and referral.
New South Wales Drug and Alcohol Authority, Level 14, McKell Building, Rawson Place, Sydney, New South Wales 2000.

Victoria
Victorian Foundation on Alcohol and Drug Dependence, PO Box 529, South Melbourne 3205.

Queensland
Alcohol and Drug Dependence Services, 'Biala', 270 Roma Street, Brisbane, Queensland 4000.

South Australia
Drug and Alcohol Services Council, 161 Greenhill Road, Parkside, South Australia 5063.

Western Australia
Western Australian Alcohol and Drug Authority, Salvatori House, 35 Outram Street, West Perth 6005.

Northern Territory
Northern Territory Drug and Alcohol Bureau, PO Box 1701, Darwin 5794.

Canada

Narcotics Anonymous Regional Service Office, 161 Princess Street West, North Bay, Ontario P1B 6C5. Check with the directory for the phone number. Quebec District Office, 1691 Champlain, Shawinigan, Quebec J9N 2K8. Check with the phone directory for the current phone number.

Alcoholics Anonymous, Suite 6, 1581 Bank Street, Ottawa, Ontario K1H 7Z3. Tel: 613 523 9977. There are phone lines for every major city, so look in your local phone directory.

Families Anonymous, PO Box 528, Van Nuys, California 91408. Tel: 213 989 7841. There are several FA meetings in Canada, but the central office is in California.

Al-anon, PO Box 182, Madison Square Station, New York, NY 10159. Tel: 212 683 1771. Check in the phone book to see if there is a local Al-anon number.

Other agencies

Alcoholism Commission of Saskatchewan, 3475 Albert Street, Regina, Saskatchewan S4S 6X6. Tel: 306–565 4085.

Alcohol and Drug Programs, Ministry of Health, 1515 Blanshard Street, Victoria, British Columbia V8V 3C8. Tel: 604 386 3166.

Nova Scotia Commission on Drug Dependency, 5675 Spring Garden Road, Halifax, Nova Scotia B3J 1H1. Tel: 902 424 4270.

Addiction Research Foundation, 33 Russell Street, Toronto, Ontario M5S 3S1. Tel: 416 595 6000.

Alcoholism Foundation of Manitoba, 1031 Portage Avenue, Winnipeg, Manitoba R3G 0R8. Tel: 204 786 3831.

Alcohol and Drug Dependency Commission, 6 Logy Bay Road, St John's, Newfoundland A1A 1J3. Tel: 709 737 3600.

Alcohol and Drug Services, Department of Health and Human Resources, Box 2703, Whitehorse, Yukon Y1A 2C6. Tel: 403 667 5777.

Addiction Services, Department of Health, PO Box 37, Charlottetown, Prince Edward Island C1A 7K2. Tel: 902 892 4265.

Alcoholism and Drug Dependency Commission of New Brunswick, 43 Brunswick Street, Fredericton, New Brunswick E3B 5H1. Tel: 506 453 2136.

Alberta Alcoholism and Drug Abuse Commission, 7th Floor, 10909 Jasper Avenue, Edmonton, Alberta T5J 3M9. Tel: 403 427 7305.

Alcohol and Drug Program, PO Box 1769, Yellowknife, Northwest Territories X1A 2L9. Tel: 403 873 7707.

New Zealand

Narcotics Anonymous. PO Box 2858, Christchurch. No fixed telephone number at the time of this book's publication in 1986. Check in your local phone book. Sometimes AA offices have an NA contact number. Or get in touch with the Narcotics Anonymous head office, 16155 Wyandotte Street, Van Nuys, California 91406. Or telephone the NA Australasian region head office in Australia: 02–810 2020.

Alcoholics Anonymous, PO Box 6458, Wellington, NI. Tel: 859 455.

Families Anonymous. In 1985 there were not yet meetings of FA in New Zealand. For up-to-date information write to Families Anonymous, PO Box 528, Van Nuys, California 91408. If your addict uses alcohol (and most do) you can get help from Al-anon.

Al-anon, Suite no 4, Charter House, 56 Customs Street, Auckland. Tel: Auckland 794-871.

Other agencies

The Drugs Advisory Committee, Department of Health, Macarthy Trust Building, Lambton Quay, Wellington. Tel: 727 627. This committee advises the Minister of Health on drug abuse. It has a list of treatment and rehabilitation centres.

South Africa

Narcotics Anonymous. In 1986 there were reports of a very small NA community in South Africa, but without an office. The main office of Alcoholics Anonymous may have a contact. If not, contact the NA World Service Office, 16155 Wyandotte Street, Van Nuys, California 91406.

Alcoholics Anonymous, PO Box 23005, Joubert Park 2044. Tel: 23 7219.

Families Anonymous. In 1985 there were no FA meetings yet in South Africa. For up-to-date information write to Families Anonymous, PO Box 528, Van Nuys, California 91408. If your addict uses alcohol (and most do) you can get help from Al-anon.

Al-anon, PO Box 2077, Johannesburg, Transvaal 2000. Tel: 011 29 6696.

Other agencies

South African National Council on Alcoholism and Drug Dependence, Happiness House, corner Loveday and Wolmarans Street, Johannesburg 2001. Tel: 011 725–5810.

Help with Specific Problems

We have listed names and addresses of organisations which may help with specific problems. But do not expect them to understand chemical dependence. Outside counsellors, ignorant of the problem, have been known to suggest to AA members that they are 'cured' or do not need AA. Ignore their advice when it conflicts with AA and NA teaching.

We have listed some campaigning organisations, because many of these have useful advice and services. Campaigners often include individuals who are full of 'righteous anger': remember that recovering addicts and alcoholics cannot afford anger, no matter how righteous the cause.

If you want advice about something which doesn't seem to be listed here, the reference section of your local library can probably help. Librarians are geared to finding out information for people. It would also be worth trying your local Citizens Advice Bureau, or even the local radio station, if the library can't help. If you are writing to any of the organisations listed below, remember to include a stamped and addressed envelope for their reply. This helps the many voluntary organisations who are short of cash.

Alternative medicine and relaxation

Acupuncture: the ancient Chinese system of medicine which works by applying hair-thin needles to specific points. British Acupuncture Association, 34 Alderney Street, London SW1V 4EU. Tel: 01–834 1012. Will supply a list of acupuncturists.

Alexander Technique: a method of re-learning posture so as to balance the body, and in particular the spine, in the right position. Society of Teachers of the Alexander Technique: 10 London House, 266 Fulham Road, London SW10 9EL. Tel: 01–351 0828.

Chiropractic: manipulation of the spine so as to realign the body in the right position. The British Chiropractic Association, 5 First Avenue, Chelmsford, Essex CM1 1RX. Tel: 0245 358487.

Hypnotherapy: hypnosis to stop smoking, help pain, etc. British Society of Medical and Dental Hypnotherapists, 42 Links Road, Ashtead, Surrey, KT21 2HJ. Will supply list of local practitioners, all qualified doctors or dentists.

Naturopathy: a combination of diet, rest, exercise and water treatments to help the body heal itself. British Naturopathic and Osteopathy Association, 6 Netherhall Gardens, London NW3. Tel: 01–435 7830.

Osteopathy: manipulation of the spine and joints to realign the body in the correct position. Usually gentler than chiropractic. Osteopaths General Council and Register, 1 Suffolk Street, London SW1Y 4HG. Tel: 01–839 2060.

Relaxation: Relaxation for Living, 29 Burwood Park Road, Walton on Thames, Surrey KT12 5LH. Relaxation classes throughout England, cassettes, leaflets and correspondence course.

Yoga: Yoga for Health Foundation, Ickwell Bury, Ickwell, Northill, Near Biggleswade, Bedfordshire SG18 9EF. Tel: 076 727 271.

Bereavement

Compassionate Friends, 6 Denmark Street, Bristol BS1 5DQ. Tel: 0272 292778. An organisation to help parents who lose a child of any age for any reason.

Cruse, the National Organisation for the Widowed and their Children, 126 Sheen Road, Richmond, Surrey TW9 1UR. Tel: 01–940 4818/9047.

Foundation for the Study of Infant Deaths. Tel: 01–235 1721 or 01–245 9421. Personal support for parents who have lost babies in cot deaths.

The Miscarriage Association, 19 Stoneybrook Close, West Bretton, Wakefield, West Yorkshire WF4 4TP. Tel: 092 485 515. Local groups give support for women who have had a miscarriage.

National Association for Widows, c/o Stafford District Voluntary Service Centre, Chell Road, Stafford ST16 2QA. Tel: 0785 45465. At the same address is the Widow's Advisory Trust, which gives help to widows with problems. Tel: 0785 58946.

Stillbirth and Neonatal Death Society, Argyle House, 29–31 Euston Road, London NW1 2FD. Tel: 01–833 2851. Support groups for parents who have lost a baby.

Relationships, sex and gender

Adult Children of Alcoholics. Some Al-anon groups are largely made up of adult children of alcoholics. Al-anon family groups, 41 Dover Street, London SE1. Tel: 01–403 0888.

Catholic Marriage Advisory Council, 15 Lansdowne Road, Holland Park, London W11 3AJ. Tel: 01–727 0141. Advises Catholics with marriage difficulties and helps with natural family planning.

Child, Farthings, Gaunts Road, Pawlet, Near Bridgwater, Somerset. Tel: 0278 683595. Self-help for couples with infertility difficulties.

Gay Switchboard. Tel: 01–837 7324. A 24-hour confidential information and advice service for homosexual men and women. The switchboard is very busy, so you may have to keep trying. If you live in a major city outside London, it may have its own gay switchboard. Look in the phone book under 'Gay'.

Gingerbread, 35 Wellington Street, London WC2. Tel: 01–240 0953. Self-help groups for one-parent families.

Incest Crisis Line, 32 Newbury Close, Northolt, Middlesex UB5 4JF. Tel: 01–422 5100 (Richard) or 01–890 4732 (Shirley). They will help with current incest problems or with the problems of those who in the past were incest victims or victims of sexual abuse. There is a network of contacts and counsellors can be recommended.

Lesbian Line. Tel: 01–251 6911. Help and advice for homosexual women.

London Friend, 274 Upper Street, London N1. Tel: 01–359 7371. Counselling for gay men and women.

National Association for the Childless, 318 Summer Lane, Birmingham B19 3RL. Tel: 021–359 4887.

National Council for One-parent Families, 255 Kentish Town Road, London NW5 2LX. Tel: 01–267 1361. Gives information and advice to one-parent families and campaigns on their behalf.

National Marriage Guidance Council, Herbert Gray College, Little Church Street, Rugby, Warwickshire CV21 3AP. Tel: 0788 73241. Counsels people about their relationships, including non-married and gay couples. Look in your local phone directory . under 'Marriage Guidance' for your local branch.

Parents Anonymous, 6–9 Manor Gardens, London N7. Tel: 01–263 8919 (for parents in difficulties) or 01–263 5672 (office). Despite its similar name, this is not a Twelve-Step organisation. It offers help for parents who are worried that they may abuse their children.

Parents Enquiry, 16 Honley Road, London SE6. Tel: 01–698 1815. Counselling for gay teenagers and their families.

Rape Crisis Centre, PO Box 69, London WC1X 9NJ. Tel: 01–837 1600 (24-hour answering service; switchboard manned 10.00 a.m. to 6.00 p.m.; answering machine gives numbers to ring after those hours) or 01–278 3956 (office). The Centre will help women who have been raped or sexually abused in the past, as well as those with current problems.

TV/TS Line. Tel: 01–359 4898. Help for transvestites, transexuals and their relatives.

Women's Aid Federation, 52–54 Featherstone Street, London EC1Y 8RY. Tel: 01–251 6537 (London) or 01–831 8581 (national office). Helps battered women and their children with advice, counselling and refuge. You may find a branch in your local phone directory.

Other problems

AIDS Helpline, Terence Higgins Trust, BN AIDS, WC1N 3XX. Tel: 01–833 2971. Help and advice about AIDS.

Anorexic Aid, The Priory Centre, 11 Priory Road, High Wycombe, Buckinghamshire. Advice and information. Groups run by ex-sufferers.

Association for Postnatal Illness, 7 Gowan Avenue, London SW6 6RH. Support for others who have suffered postnatal depression.

Back Pain Association, 31–33 Park Road, Teddington, Middlesex. Tel: 01–977 5474. Leaflets, books and local branches.

Bacup, British Association of Cancer United Patients, 121–123 Charterhouse Street, London EC1M 6AA. Tel: 01–608 1661. Information about cancer for patients, families and friends.

Foresight, The Old Vicarage, Church Lane, Witley, Godalming, Surrey GU8 5PN. Helps with pre-conception planning and advises on the best way to conceive a healthy child.

Gamblers Anonymous, 17–23 Blantyre Street, London SW10. Tel: 01–352 3060. A Twelve-Step programme for those who gamble compulsively. For partners and families of gamblers there is Gam-Anon at the same address and phone number. Look in the local phone book to see if a local GA number is listed.

Mastectomy Association, 26 Harrison Street, off Gray's Inn Road, London WC1H 8JG. Tel: 01–837 0908. Practical advice and help from women who have had mastectomies.

National Childbirth Trust, 9 Queensborough Terrace, London W2 3TB. Tel: 01–221 3833. Antenatal and postnatal courses. Leaflets on relaxation techniques.

Overeaters Anonymous, Manor Gardens Centre, 6–9 Manor Gardens, London N7 6LA. Tel: 01–868 4109. A Twelve-Step programme for people with overeating problems.

Samaritans, 17 Uxbridge Road, Slough, Berkshire SL1 1SN. Tel: 01 75 32713. For the Samaritan phone service in your area look in the local phone book. If it's late at night, you don't know whom to ring, and you feel desperate, the Samaritans are there to talk to you. They help those who feel that life is getting too much to bear and also can help relatives of those who have committed suicide.

Tranx, Tranquilliser Recovery and New Existence, 17 Peel Road, Harrow, Middlesex HA3 7QX. Tel: 01–427 2065. Help and advice for those who may be dependent on tranquillisers and sleeping pills. May help you find a local self-help group. Also look in your local phone book under 'Tranx' or 'Tranquilliser' for other groups.

Recommended Reading

AA and NA books

Alcoholics Anonymous. The so-called 'Big Book' written by the first hundred founders of AA, and published by AA.
Twelve Steps and Twelve Traditions. How members of AA recover and how the society functions, published by AA. Write to the AA national office (address in Appendix 2) for a literature order form.

Narcotics Anonymous. Written by the members of NA and published by NA. Write to the NA national office or to the World Service office (addresses in Appendix 2) for a literature order form.

Alateen: Hope for Children of Alcoholics. Published by Al-anon. Write to the Al-anon national office (address in Appendix 2) for a literature order form.
The Dilemma of the Alcoholic Marriage. Published by Al-anon. Write to the Al-anon national office (address in Appendix 2) for a literature order form.

Other books

Bethune, Helen, *Off the Hook: Coping with Addiction*, Methuen, London 1985.

Cutland, Liz, *Kick Heroin*, Gateway Books, London, 1985.

Gold, Mark S., *800-Cocaine*, Bantam Books, New York, 1984.

Haddon, Celia, *Women and Tranquillisers*, Sheldon Press, London, 1984.

*Hafen, Brent Q., and Fransden, Kathryn J., *Marijuana: Facts, Figures and Information for the 1980s*, Hazelden, Center City, Minnesota, 1980.

*Hafner, A. Jack, *It's Not as Bad as You Think: Coping with Upset Feelings*, Hazelden, Center City, Minnesota, 1981.

*Kurtz, Ernest, *Not God: a History of Alcoholics Anonymous*, Hazelden, Center City, Minnesota, 1979.

**Maxwell, Ruth, *The Booze Battle*, Ballantine, New York, 1976.

**Rice Drews, Toby, *Getting Them Sober, Vols. 1 and 2*, Bridge Publishing, South Plainfield, New Jersey, 1980, 1983.

*Van Almen, W. J., *500 Drugs the Alcoholic Should Avoid*, Hazelden, Center City, Minnesota, 1983.

Young, Howard, S., *A Rational Counselling Primer*, Institute for Rational–Emotive Therapy, New York, 1974.

*Books can be ordered direct from Hazelden Educational Services, Box 176, Center City, Mn 55012. Tel: 612–257–4010. You can pay by international money order or by international credit card.

**A wide variety of books on alcoholism, including the Hazelden publications, is stocked by A. J. Stoyel, 329 Addiscombe Road, Croydon, Surrey.

Index